Edmund H. Sears

Sermons and Songs of Christian Life

Edmund H. Sears

Sermons and Songs of Christian Life

ISBN/EAN: 9783337516420

Printed in Europe, USA, Canada, Australia, Japan

Cover: Foto ©Lupo / pixelio.de

More available books at **www.hansebooks.com**

SERMONS AND SONGS

OF

THE CHRISTIAN LIFE.

BY

EDMUND H. SEARS,

AUTHOR OF "THE HEART OF CHRIST," "REGENERATION,"
AND "FOREGLEAMS OF IMMORTALITY."

BOSTON:
NOYES, HOLMES, AND COMPANY,
219 WASHINGTON STREET.
PHILADELPHIA:
CLAXTON, REMSEN, AND HAFFELFINGER.
1875.

TO THE

THREE CHRISTIAN SOCIETIES

IN

LANCASTER, WAYLAND, AND WESTON,

IN WHOSE SERVICE THESE SERMONS WERE FIRST PREPARED, AND WITH WHOM I HAVE HELD PASTORAL RELATIONS, FRAUGHT WITH THE MEMORIES OF HAPPY YEARS,

𝕋his volume

IS MOST GRATEFULLY INSCRIBED.

PREFACE.

THE discourses comprised in this volume have been selected with special reference to those days observed by the Christian Church in commemoration of the fundamental facts of the Gospel history, and to the Christian life and experience which grow from a living apprehension of the system of truth which rests upon them. I do not regard it as the province of the Sermon to go behind the facts themselves, or try to prove them. That belongs to works of another kind. The Sermon assumes them as premises acknowledged by the congregation, and prophesies from them, but in such wise and with such applications to the wants of the human heart, as to complement the historical evidence with the clearest spiritual vision and the most assured experience of Christian believers. This in itself is evidence, and without it the historical facts are of little avail, and finally lose their hold, even upon the intellect, notwithstanding the completeness of the historic demonstration.

In our church service the Sermon consummates in the hymn, or sacred song, which makes the heart lyrical with the truth it sets forth. The idea that the sentiment which inspires the hymn is a hindrance to exact criticism, or the clearest and truest interpretation of the record, I resist as false in theory, and proved abundantly so in practice. A plodding criticism keeps close to the earth, and fails to see the significance of some of the most large and positive affirmations of the Gospel narrative, and so pares them away and reduces the whole Christian Revelation within the compass of our earthly vision. The best and most trustworthy historians are men who have enough of the imaginative faculty to reproduce the past as it really lived; and the best commentators have been men whose intuitions were large and deep enough to bring them into some correspondency with the Mind that inspired the letter, so that they may not merely dig over the surface of the letter itself.

Without claiming these qualifications, I would only say that I had written at different times several lyrical pieces which were afloat in collections of hymns, or in periodicals, sometimes altered and mutilated. I have brought them together in this volume, some of them revised and amended, some of them simply restored, and I have added others not before published. As they are more or less adapted to the subjects of the discourses, and help to give the truths which they handle a fullness of utterance, I have interspersed them, like the hymns in the Sunday Service, though some of them are lyrics rather than hymns. The song, or hymn, should be a summing up of the sermon, helping us to take home its truth, and so carry it with us as to fill our daily life with its melodies. I hesitated long in regard to some of these songs, because they are flavored so much with personal experience; but this is true of most of the hymns that speak to the condition of others, and as best advised, I concluded to put them in, trusting to the large indulgence of my readers.

The Sermons were written, not for the press, but the pulpit, and are given mainly as they were delivered. I should revise them a good deal more if I sought to reduce them to the standard of classical taste, but I believe in that way they would lose in point and directness; and so I dismiss them as they are, hoping they will find a response in the hearts of some readers worthy of the themes which they set forth.

I believe every Christian should have church relations, and be faithful to them, and I have always studied to render faithful service to the denomination where a good Providence placed me; not by trying to conform to the average opinions which may be current among them to-day, but by trying to grasp and bring forth anew the vital truths essential alike to individual progress and denominational life. For when brought face to face with the central truths of Christianity, the idea of sect merges in the larger conception of the Church Universal, with Christ for its living Head and daily inspiration. I believe the best service which any man can render his denomination is to help on a consummation like this ; and this I would do in perfect loyalty to the branch of the Church to which it is my privilege to belong, and as some return for the large freedom of opinion and utterance which they have vouchsafed and defended. The time I believe is not far off when there is to be larger freedom in every branch of the Christian Zion for the treatment and readjustment of the great truths of Religion, and that this freedom is to consummate, not in new divisions, but in broader and warmer fellowship, and a more perfect and comprehending unity. For it will be a unity not imposed from without, but a growth within, from more intelligent convictions and the deeper inspirations of the Spirit which comes through these convictions themselves. E. H. S.

CONTENTS.

SERMONS.

		PAGE
I.	The Cloud of Witnesses	1
II.	One Mediator	19
III.	The Will-power	35
IV.	Calvary	51
V.	Resurrection and Ascension	67
VI.	Intercessions of the Spirit	85
VII.	The Gospel Contrasts	99
VIII.	Treading the Wine-press	117
IX.	The New Creation	135
X.	Concerning Death	149
XI.	The Universal Redemption	167
XII.	The Box of Ointment	183
XIII.	No more Sea	199
XIV.	The Christian Church as a Means of Progress	219
XV.	Ideals of Womanhood	239
XVI.	The Divine Life-plan	259
XVII.	Home	279
XVIII.	Heavenly Treasures	297
XIX.	The Immediate Knowledge of God	319

SONGS AND HYMNS.

Christmas Carols	17
Christmas Song	33
Peace, be Still	49
The Twisted Thorn	65
A Song of Victory	81

CONTENTS.

	PAGE
THE THREE ADVENTS	97
A SONG IN THE MINOR KEY	115
THE SILENT PRAYER	131
THE NEW MORNING	147
LITTLE WILLIE WAKING UP	163
THE YOUNG HUNTER	181
IDEALS	197
PARTED	215
NOT LOST BUT RISEN	216
SONG FOR THE COMING CRISIS	235
HYMN FOR THE PLYMOUTH CELEBRATION	237
GIRLHOOD AND WOMANHOOD	255
ABOVE THE STORMS	275
"FEED MY LAMBS"	293
GLAD WORSHIP	294
I WANT NO FLOWERS	295
VESPER HYMN	296
CHAMBERS OF IMAGERY	313

SERMONS AND SONGS.

I.

THE CLOUD OF WITNESSES.

(PREACHED ALL-SAINTS DAY.)

HEBREWS xii. 1. *Seeing we also are compassed about with so great a cloud of witnesses, let us lay aside every weight, and the sin which doth so easily beset us, and let us run with patience the race that is set before us.*

THE writer of this book, called "the Epistle to the Hebrews," is not known with any certainty. There is no question, however, that it is a genuine production of the primitive Church, written by one of the contemporaries of the Apostles, and that it reflects the mind of the early believer before Christianity had been corrupted by pagan philosophy. The book has a unity and plan which are very striking, and it sets forth the apostolic doctrine with much fervor and perspicuity.

In the chapter from which I take the text, and indeed the whole chapter preceding, the writer sets forth the doctrine of angels. He goes back and enumerates a long train of martyrs who have passed up to the skies, some of them through the baptism of blood and fire. These, he reminds his readers, are a witness-train, and he refers to them as if they were still looking on; a vast company that girds them round to help them gain the victory. His doctrine seems to be, Ye are acting in no obscure corner. All the ranks above are looking on. You stand at the centre of an immense amphitheatre. Row beyond row they are watching you. "Ye are come unto Mount Zion, to the city of the living God; to the heavenly Jerusalem; to an innumerable company of angels; to the general assembly of the church of the first-born which are written in heaven; to the spirits of good men made perfect; and to God the judge of all." He does not refer to these merely as examples. Those who have put on immortality he calls elsewhere "ministering spirits sent forth to minister for them who shall be heirs of salvation." Such, as we gather from no obscure intimations in the Acts and in Paul's writings, and from the words of the Master himself, was the primitive Christian doctrine of guardian angels. I need not say what courage and what earnest of victory it gave to the early converts to Christianity. It was as if countless tiers of faces were looking down, turning aside in grief if they faltered and failed; and as if hands multitudinous as the waves clapped together and cheered them on at every victory they achieved.

This admirable Christian philosophy, or rather pneumatology, became corrupted. It degenerated into saint-worship and thence into image-worship. In this way, by about the seventh century, the old paganism under new names had been imported into the very heart of the Church and the worship of pictures and statues entered largely into the cultus of Christendom. The fiercest struggle of the eighth century arose from an attempt of the Greek Emperor to reform the paganism of the Church and break the images. It was in vain. The people rose up everywhere in rebellion against the edicts. "I am too poor," writes one of the bishops, "to possess books. I have no leisure for reading. I enter a church choked with the cares of the world; the glowing colors attract my sight and delight my eyes like a flowery meadow, and the glory of God steals imperceptibly into my soul. I gaze on the fortitude of the martyr and the crown with which he is rewarded, and the fire of holy enthusiasm kindles within me, and I fall down and worship God, and through the martyr receive salvation."

It was the abuse of a doctrine educed from the deep wants of the human heart. Protestantism should have respected the doctrine itself and cleared it of idolatrous perversion. But the reformers of the sixteenth century swept away not only the corruptions but the doctrine along with them; so that our denuded Protestantism looks up and finds the witness-train all vanished from sight and a blank space between us and the naked heavens.

The cloud of witnesses! We will endeavor to bring out the primitive Christian doctrine and show its practical use, power, and influence. That this innumerable train of witnesses are spectators of all that we do, or even have cognizance of our external life, would be a construction altogether too literal, avouched neither by Scripture nor reason. Only the Omniscient eye sees all our actions and all states of mind and affection ere yet they have ripened into conduct. In quite other methods, however, the witness-train may beset us and engird us, and be a more mighty incentive to us than they could become as outside witnesses or lookers-on.

The general doctrine as I apprehend it is this, — that the spirit-world and this are continuous and interblending and from that run down into this the influence and energy on which we draw mightily in our struggles and conquests; that no man is alone or isolated; that there are chords of sympathy that run from us along the higher ranks of being; that the repentance of a single sinner is an event that sends a wavelet of joy into the breasts of those who have been an invisible guard around his virtue and helped determine his decision for the right.[1] The universe is related part to part, visible and invisible. There are laws of attraction pertaining to mind

[1] See Luke xv. 7, 10.

and spirit as well as matter, which no gulfs of space can suspend or abolish, so that no portion is broken off from any other portion; but there are fine threads of nerve which run through the whole and make a calamity in one part a calamity to all. But let me illustrate and break the general doctrine into its specialties. The cloud of witnesses may be manifest and affect us in one or all of three ways:—

To sight, or external senses;
To faith made rational and clear;
To the heart made peaceful and strong.

I. There may be disclosures of immortality to our grosser perceptions; I will not say to the bodily senses, but to the senses that lie close within them and are sheathed by them, and which before death as well as after may have open converse with higher things. This is only saying that we are already immortal beings and belong to a higher sphere than this earthly one. This, however, is not the sort of disclosure which the Scriptures refer to when they speak of the company of the witness-train. This writer to the Hebrews does not mean that we are connected by sense with them nor they with us, for he puts into the same enumeration Jesus the Mediator of the New Covenant and God the Judge of all. The reasons against any such connection as this, as a normal condition of our present being, are obvious enough. A sentient connection with spheres of being where our duties do not lie would not enlarge and strengthen but repress our higher and nobler manhood. Even now and here the continual problem is how to keep the sense faculties from becoming so luxuriant as to overtop and repress the reason. They are the most seductive, the most bewildering, the most lying of all our faculties, unless educated and subordinated and their impressions constantly corrected and verified by the rational powers. The infant, when his senses first open upon this world, sees all its objects projected confusedly upon one ground, and he must learn by experience the laws of perspective. It took five thousand years of unfolding reason to reverse the verdict of the senses which reported the universe inside out and upside down. Men of science tell us at this day that descriptions of phenomena by unscientific observers are unreliable and nearly worthless for all the purposes of science. For yet stronger reasons, if in this childhood of our being the spirit-world were given to our senses, it would give us phenomena rather than the higher realities; appearances rather than the laws that underlie them — those eternal and universal laws which in the book of Divine Revelation are addressed to a higher and worthier part of our nature. Even when our spiritual senses are first unsheathed and the eternal substances are about us, it seems probable from all analogy that appearances will lie upon us adaptive and tender, and melt away or disclose the laws that govern them, as our higher nature unfolds and is prepared for the eternal verities in their unclouded glory.

For yet higher reasons the witness-train are not manifest to our senses. Hero-worship in this world is a very dangerous kind of homage, tending to draw out of the worshipper the prime principles of manhood and waft incense to the pride and vanity of the hero. Saint-worship is more dangerous still, and would become sheer idolatry if we had visible connection and intercourse with the witness-train — for among that train are your own kinsfolk, to whom your hearts went out in their warmest love, and to whom in their glorified being the affections yearn with a fervor which time does not cool, but fans, rather, into more burning flame. If they appeared above you they would fill the void till the Father's face were shut out from view, and you would need constantly the voice of the rebuking angel — "See thou do it not!" Hence the guards, the warnings, the denunciations interposed throughout the old Bible, and repeated in the new, against the necromancy that would substitute "familiar spirits" for the Spirit of the Lord, or take reports from them as a revelation from heaven.

II. There was a man, nevertheless, who appeared in this world with all the wants and susceptibilities of our human nature, and so endowed at the same time with the presence and indwelling of the Godhead, that none of these dangers beset Him. He dwelt "in heaven" and on the earth at the same time. Not alone the words of Jesus but his life is a revelation to us on this as on kindred themes. The full import of the words, that He "brought immortality to light," will appear to you as you follow Him from Bethlehem to Ascension Mount. This life divides itself into four of its grander epochs, representing the periods corresponding to it in every human probation on the earth — his birth, his temptation, his death, and his return to his place on high. At each of these events the clouds disappear from the heights and show the heavens touching the earth, and the cloud of witnesses transfusing celestial energy through its affairs. The song over Bethlehem was the quiring of "the young-eyed cherubim," whose melodies have never died away since the morning stars sang together, but whose chant then and there was so strong and triumphant that it broke audibly through the discords of earth. The angels that "came and ministered" unto Jesus after his great victory over temptation, disclose one of the sources of that ineffable peace, falling as it were from hovering and protecting wings, vouchsafed to every follower of Christ when he triumphs over evil and sin. The valley of the shadow of death through which Jesus passed, lay between the Mount of Transfiguration and the open sepulchre of resurrection morning. The witness-train were visible on the mount, in Gethsemane, and at the sepulchre; they were close on the other side as the divinely appointed guard shining through the rents in this veil of mortality. And on Ascension Mount they appear again. Do you say that all this was miracle? Undoubtedly it was; but you may forget that miracle is not the breaking of law, but the revelation thereof giving us fragmentary gleams of the vast system of agencies and workings whose unveiled operation would bewilder and amaze us. The weak, tempted, suffering nature of Jesus was like all other human natures. He came not to save Himself but to save humanity; to lift up our faith into serener light; to take up our experience into his own, and show openly at the same time the helps and the guards that are always nigh. His experience would not be ours, unless the helps and the guards were ours as well as the trials and the sufferings. Not as the Eternal Creative Word, not as the God-with-us did He need the angelic ministries, but as a sharer in our common humanity; and as such He opens vistas to us of the cloud of witnesses that surround us, when to break down the separating wall would make sure an invasion we could never bear.

If not to the senses, then yet to faith made rational and clear the witness train is disclosed. This is what the writer specially means. He has just given an admirable description of this faculty of faith. He calls it the substance (ὑπόστασις) of things hoped for, the demonstration of things not seen. That is to say, faith made open and clear apprehends its objects as the real substances beyond the shifting panorama of sight. Faith has the demonstration or higher beholding of things invisible to mortal eyes. He appeals here to a power within us which, being divinely touched and illumined, lays hold of its objects and possesses them with an assurance beyond that of sight. Jesus not only had disclosures of immortality, but He gives interpretations thereof, and reveals the laws and the substance that underlie them. Without these interpretations the disclosures of the spirit-world would only come to us as " apparitions," and so the world generally has agreed to call them. Sight only gives us phenomena ; faith made clear and rational gives us what lies within the phenomena, and is the ground and substance of all its exflorations.

Illustrate. Look at the mazy round of night and day, and even and morn, and suns and stars in their courses! How different to the child who only sees appearances and the man of reason who sees what is within them, and judges not from phenomena but from eternal and shining laws. So of faith made rational and clear. To our higher reason God may so reveal to us the things of the higher life, may make the laws of spiritual existence so radiant and all harmonizing, so rounded and complete, both to the intellect and the heart, that the eternal world shall be mirrored down to us here in time as it never could be by any fragmentary disclosures to our timid and wildering senses. And when this is so, faith has the substance of things hoped for, the demonstration and beholding of things to come, just as they will be found when we pass into them down into the depths of the endless years! Hence it was that these first Christians acted as in presence of the great realities. Those realities broke upon their faith with a power and certitude which sense even could not give, so that on the cross and in the fire this world of shows faded out altogether, and the city of the living God, the heavenly Jersalem, the myriads of angels in full assembly, the spirits of good men perfected, Jesus the mediator and God over all, — these rose in brightening ranks and filled all the firmanent of vision as the substahce of things hoped for, and of which all things else are but the earnest and the shadow.

III. But higher yet, and still farther inward, are manifestations to us of the cloud of witnesses — namely, to the heart made peaceful and strong.

It is, I believe, a law of spiritual being, that there are bonds which are subtile and pervasive, and which join the body of true disciples as a living and organic whole, so that

"The church on earth and all the dead
But one communion make."

This, in fact, is the doctrine of the New Testament,

and this is the true Catholic Church, standing complete in its beauty before the eye of the Lord, every part joined vitally to every other part, each receiving the currents of life from all the rest, and being thus swept mightily along. There are two kinds of energy by which the Lord draws us up into his peaceful heavens. One is communion with Himself, or prayer, the other is that energy called in the Apostle's Creed "the communion of saints." These last words have come to mean little or nothing in our rationalizing Protestantism that crumbles everything into individualism. In the primitive Church they meant that every true believer was included vitally in one great Catholicity, in which he was pervaded by the common consciousness, and by which the life of all the saints above and below flowed into him. And this is none other than the fulfillment of the prayer of Christ: "Holy Father, keep through thine own name those whom thou hast given me, that they may be one as we are. As thou, Father, art in me and I in thee, that they also may be one in us, that the world may believe that thou hast sent me." And death has no power to make any rents or breaks in this communion and this unity. It is the sphere of mind flowing into mind, and heart into heart; and inasmuch as death cleaves away our clumsy clogs and hindrances, these interactions are more perfect than before. The Saviour said, "If I go away I will come again;" that is, come nearer than ever. This is that Church catholic in which human popedoms have no power of excommunication, for it is drawn into unity, not by outward distinctions and priestly rules, but by inward fitness and regeneration. Hence, with every evil overcome, and every new likeness of Christ inwardly put on, you are brought more completely within the circle of the great cloud of witnesses, the myriads of angels in full assembly, and the spirits of good men made perfect; their strength passes mightily into your soul and their peace is laid brightly within the heart. This is one of the essential elements of our strength when we are supported and buoyed up in doing the Divine will. You are not marching alone. You feel it; you know it. Visible or invisible, a mighty host is with you; you are marching with them in countless and serried numbers; one spirit moves the whole and lifts their feet, and they keep step to the same music. If we are with the right and for it, though all the world have gone over to the other side, the long line of ancestral and glorified men are behind us and breathing upon us,

"Troops of beautiful tall angels to enshield us from all wrong."

If they came to us from without, if they came to our timid senses, they would repress our manhood and overlay it; taking the place of our reason and leading us servilely after them. But now they build us up within, their celestial energy we make our own; we appropriate it by our rational and voluntary life, and so put it on as our robe and diadem.

How impressively this subject appeals to us now! We have just closed four years of trial during which thousands of martyrs, the flower of the country, have given up their lives to save it.[1] In the light of my subject, death has not taken them from us, but given them to us, and their spirit is to inspire our Future and help to unfold it. For the more of good men that rise up to the place of ancestors, the more mighty is the influence that comes invisibly from the witness-train. Yea, the more consciously and swiftly will the earth and the heavens become one. What a privilege, in this view of the matter, to live in such times as these! And how animating the thought that as the heavens fill up and bend over us more nearly, the more virtue comes down to the earth and the swifter its redemption draweth nigh!

The subject abounds with incitements to the Christian life which are full of encouragement. It takes us out of the little cliques and parties of the day, and places us among the blest societies of all ages. It raises us out of sect and puts us peacefully within the church universal, embracing the firstborn which are written in heaven and the last good man that went up into its pale. Your home may be humble, apart, alone; but if a good life is lived there,

[1] This sermon was preached in 1865.

it stands in the centre of an amphitheatre thronged with heavenly multitudes, all bending towards you and breathing their spirit into yours. Nearest about you are those of like character, like trials, and like victories, who have conquered through just such a path as yours, and whose life beats through you with every step that is gained. Farther up are the lengthening ranges, the clouds of witnesses, and looking down through all and breathing through all, is Christ the Mediator of the new covenant and God the Judge of all. Only remember the condition by which you put on the strength and are swept by the spirit of this goodly multitude, — "laying aside every weight, and the sin that doth so easily beset us, and running with patience the race that is set before us, ever looking to Jesus the author and finisher of our faith."

CHRISTMAS CAROLS.

IT came upon the midnight clear,
  That glorious song of old,
From angels bending near the earth
  To touch their harps of gold;
"Peace on the earth, good will to men
  From heaven's all-gracious King"—
The world in solemn stillness lay
  To hear the angels sing.

Still through the cloven skies they come
  With peaceful wings unfurled,
And still their heavenly music floats
  O'er all the weary world;
Above its sad and lowly plains
  They bend on hovering wing,
And ever o'er its Babel-sounds
  The blessed angels sing.

But with the woes of sin and strife
  The world has suffered long;
Beneath the angel-strain have rolled
  Two thousand years of wrong;
And man, at war with man, hears not
  The love-song which they bring;—
Oh hush the noise, ye men of strife,
  And hear the angels sing!

And ye, beneath life's crushing load,
    Whose forms are bending low,
Who toil along the climbing way
    With painful steps and slow,
Look now! for glad and golden hours
    Come swiftly on the wing; —
Oh, rest beside the weary road
    And hear the angels sing!

For lo! the days are hastening on
    By prophet bards foretold,
When with the ever circling years
    Comes round the age of gold;
When Peace shall over all the earth
    Its ancient splendors fling,
And the whole world give back the song
    Which now the angels sing.

II.

ONE MEDIATOR.

(CHRISTMAS EVE.)

1 TIMOTHY ii. 6. *There is one God and one Mediator between God and men, the man Christ Jesus.*

THE word here rendered "Mediator" means one who comes between two parties, and, in the more specific Christian sense of the word, between two parties to reconcile them and make peace between them. It presupposes a state of emnity and warfare, so that an old commentator does no more than justice to the original when he renders — There is one God, and one peace-maker between God and man.

We do not yet, however, come to the full thought of the original word. These analogies from human affairs only help us a little to climb up to the great doctrine involved. A man who goes between two hostile armies and negotiates a peace, represents very dimly and remotely the Divine Mediation in Jesus Christ. On the Divine side this does not represent the fact at all. For God has no hostility towards his creatures; the enmity is all on one side, and the fearful chasm and antagonism between the Divine nature and human nature do not require any treaty-making or going between, that God may understand us, and be made placable towards us. The thing needed is not an arbitrator to settle disputed points, but a channel rather through which the Divine life and energy can flow. Suppose this Mediator, then, not merely to come between the two parties, but to embody the whole spirit and moral power of the rightful one, — that these possess Him, and clothe Him with their majesty and grace, — that thus He comes to the hostile party on their own ground and among their own camp-fires, and dissolves their hatred beneath the touches of his own spirit, and that then they throw down their arms and strike their banners and say we are reconciled and we will rebel no more. This will give more completely the burden of the text, "there is one God and one Peace-maker between God and man." He is peace-maker in that he opens between both the streams and courses through which the Divine Peace flows to man and reconciles him, so to say, under the Omnipotence of the Divine Love.

The prime necessity of a Mediator is not because God needs to be appeased or reconciled, but because He does require means and instrumentalities to reach the lowest of his children. Think of the distance between the Infinite God and finite and feeble man! He cannot come to us in his unveiled and eternal essence, for then we should drop senseless into the deeps of his own absolute Being. So He veils that essence and accommodates it to the state of all the creatures He has made. It were not enough, again, that God come to us through the motions of his Spirit within us. We are sinful, sensuous, dark, liable all the while to mistake God's motions within us, in our own noxious, smouldering passions. There must be, then, not only the light within — there must also be the light without and above; there must be the objective manifestation of the Deity.

But observe, again, what an emphasis Paul lays on this *oneness* of the mediatorial office. There can be only one mediator even as there can be only one God. Indeed he puts one as the correlate of the other. For he means to say, There is only one God and only one peace-maker between God and man. How and why this is so we shall see by drawing out the three propositions involved in the text, and see at the same time the amplitude and grandeur of this fundamental truth of the New Testament.

There must be one mediator.

And he must be a man.

And a man in the supreme sense — the man Christ Jesus.

There is only one — but why not? Why not make all things the media through which God comes to man, — all nature, all good men, all spirits and angels? Is not the whole universe a system of mediation through which God seeks to impart Himself to his children? Does He not come in the springtime, in the May-flowers that open their eyes upon us out of his own gentleness and beauty? And does He not speak out of his majesty in the thunder and the storm? Does He not come to us out of every pure heart and all pure lips that have a gospel to tell us? And does He not come in the angels that guard us and encamp round about us?

Yes; but does He come in these or in all together in the sense asserted by the text; not only as mediators, but as peace-givers? Are these the channels through which the Divine Peace-giver comes in to wash the cells of the heart and cool the fever of heart and brain. That nature is no such mediation as this, is obvious enough if you will look at the facts of the case and not take the dreams of sentimentalists for realities. Nature is no direct and perfect medium of the Divine character and essence. It is an exhibition to us, doubtless, in a lower degree of God's ideals of the good, the perfect, and the fair, but an exhibition as well of the condition and moods of sinful and imperfect men. All that man is casts its shadow on the dial-plate of nature, — a shadow sometimes most portentous and baleful. Convulsions, storms, deformities, miasmas, disease, death, corruption, — these are all involved in the processes of nature, these come in as contrasts to the peace and the paler beauty which are also there. Nature is the thought of God, say some of the scientists. But God's thought about what, and under what conditions?

It is God's thought obscured and dimmed and inverted sometimes ere it gets to its ultimations in the material universe. Do you suppose He would create the wolves, the tigers, the vermin, and the reptiles, the noisome things that swarm into life, as the exhibition of *his* thoughts? Even the clear skies with drought and frost, May mornings with east winds, winter with its damps and chills, are hardly the supreme beauty unveiled and clear, but struggling rather through media that obscure it. Any one of you can imagine a fairer nature than the one we have. Everything indicates that nature in its completeness is not so much the highest ideal of God as the reflection and representation of man, — all that is good in him and all that is bad copied out of him; both heaven and hell painted on the canvas that hangs around him, and showing him the grace and sweetness of the one and the deformities and stormful agencies of the other. Hence nature alone, since the world began, never has been any such mediation as yields God to man in his supreme perfections, but dimmed by the medium itself.

I should follow precisely the same line of argument touching the mediation of good men. None are good enough to stand between me and the supreme excellency without refracting it, or, worse yet, casting their shadow instead of transmitting the light. Saints, philanthropists, and martyrs are mediators to us in a quite inferior sense, and as such we thank God that He raises them up. They come between God and the fallen and the lost; they bring precious gifts from Him; they bring kindly sympathies, holy charities, words of cheer. The Divine Grace sometimes gets reflected from them in its sweeter charms. But they too are sinful like you and me, and they are no such peace-makers between God and the sinner as the text describes. They are no such channels as God yields Himself through, in the tidal fullness of his renewing love. They have struggled with sin like the rest of us, and are struggling yet; yea, they have felt precisely the need which the text indicates — and they feel it now — the need of one peace-maker between God and man, through whom the Divine peace itself shall come like a river and make human nature at one with the Divine. There is the mediation of angels, the "cloud of witnesses" I have just described, the heavens that bend near us and out of which the heavenly peace comes down into our hearts. But at the head of this witness-train, as you remember, is "Jesus the Mediator of the new covenant," made objectively to the Church and the world the revelation of the Divine attributes and the impersonation of the eternal love so that the ministry of angels is in no danger of becoming a mere spiritism taking sides with our selfish passions or wildering fancies, but is merged and included in the higher and broader ministries of the Son of God.

Only one mediator, and he is human. And why must he be a man? Simply because God is human and nothing else than humanity can transmit Him as He is. This grand truth of the HUMANITY OF GOD, rightly discriminated and apprehended, is one of the most precious and vital in all the treasury of the Gospel. It is opposed to two specious and besetting errors, that God is an impassive force somewhere at the centre of things, whence this great mechanism of worlds grew out by spontaneous evolution, — and it is opposed to the more hideous notion that He is an arbitrary sovereign. In the place of either it brings out the doctrine that God is a being who like us has feelings, desires, yearnings, yea *wants*, for He wants to impart his own peace, and gain from his creatures some returns for his infinite love. Open your Bible and see how directly you are drawn away from the old stoicism that God reposes on the peaks of eternity cold and serene, leaving the world with their mean affairs to inferior deities. In the Bible we read of Divine humanities, Divine griefs and sorrows, as if the Divine sympathies ran down through all sensitive beings and felt every pulse of woe in his universe. I cannot see the Scripture or the reason of the proposition which some of our theologians have striven to make good — that God is incapable of suffering. As if that were perfection! What would you think of a man who sought to become perfect by becoming impassive and turning himself into stone? As man becomes better and more godlike he becomes more susceptible to the sorrows of his fellows, and makes their griefs his griefs, and in this very susceptibility he ascends to a bliss altogether more sacred and plenary than these men of wood and granite, that never suffer at all. And whence does all this susceptibility come to us? It comes out of the heart of God. It is a trait of the Divine Nature transcribed into man. It tells us that there are sufferings which are Divine; and that the more our natures become open to them the more we become changed into the likeness of our glorious original. Thus we speak of the Divine Compassion, and that means suffering with another, so that in our spontaneous speech we belie our wretched pagan theologies. And as if description by words were not enough, St. John in apocalyptic vision looks away up to the throne of God and what does he see there? Not an arbitrary sovereign clothed in pomp and terror, not the lightnings out of the storm-clouds, not the show of magnificence affected by earthly sovereigns — but right in the midst of the throne, as it were getting sight of the Heart of God, *a lamb as it had been slain* — the wounded love of the Creator himself, as if there was a Calvary not in Palestine alone but away in the Heart of God, where we crucify Him by our disobedience every day.

This being so, how plain it becomes that only Humanity can mediate between man and the Divine Essence. Nature is competent to evolve his power and magnificence; we feel that sensibly enough when she crushes us like insects out of her way, or brushes us by the hundred into her great gulf-stream, but in all her gamut she has not a single tone that is *human* or which can give us one lisp of the humanity of God. Nature in her impotency and her failure, man in his most urgent wants, point alike to this grand necessity, that there shall be a mediator, and that that mediator shall be a man.

And not any or every man, but THE MAN CHRIST JESUS; a man whose nature opens both ways — up to God on the Divine side, and down to the lowest of us on the human; not some tall angel talking to us from a distance out of the porches of heaven, but some one clothed in our nature, touching the earth in its lowest place of evil and darkness, and at the same time touching the inmost heaven where all the Divine scenery lay upon his soul; not sinful humanity, that cuts off the light rather than transmits it, but one supremely perfect, through whose translucency the whole Divine Nature is imaged forth. "Believest thou not that I am in the Father and the Father in me? The words that I speak unto you I speak not of myself, but the Father that dwelleth in me He doeth the works." " I in them and they in me, that they also may be made perfect in one, and that the world may know that thou hast sent me." "All things are delivered unto me of my Father, and no man knoweth the Son but the Father, neither knoweth any man the Father save the Son and he to whomsoever the Son will reveal Him. Come unto me all ye that labor and are heavy laden and I will give you rest." These proofs and illustrations show yet more openly the Divine burden of truth which the text brings home to us, — one God and one peace-maker between God and men, the man Christ Jesus.

And what is the peace from God which comes through this mediation?

First we say, peace of mind, rest from those tossings of controversy for which there is no umpire or final appeal. "Ye call me Master and Lord, and ye say well, for so I am." Human reason, after its guessings and roamings from sect to sect, yearns for a Lord and a Master, not to crush it down but to take it up, weak, bewildered, and weary, and fold it in that Divine Reason whence alone it borrows vigor and illumination. Here is rest from the trials of faith, peace from the janglings of sect, assurance after the twilight gleams of our own intuitions. If you have been through the circuit of guess-work after truth, and like the man lost in boundless woods, come back at evening to the spot you left in the morning, you will find how sweet is the intellectual repose in the Reason of God or the Word made flesh. "I have wandered long and far," says one of these men, "but have not found the rest which you say is to be obtained. I have interrogated my own soul, but it answers not. I have gazed upon nature, but its many voices speak no articulate language to *me;* and more especially when I gaze on the bright page of the midnight heavens, those orbs gleam upon me with so cold a light and amid a silence so portentous, that I am terrified with the spectacle of the infinite solitude." To the intellect weary with its wanderings, and with no God-ward determinations, appeals the doctrine of one God and one peace-maker between God and man. I do not mean by this that repose in the Christian atonement, or faith in the Christian revelation, forbids or supersedes investigation, doubt, denial, and the most careful balancing of evidence. No; doubt if you must, deny if you must, weigh the arguments in the nicest intellectual scales. The clearest affirmation comes after doubt; but alas for the inquiries that end in nothing; alas for the search after truth that goes down in darkness; alas for the gropings after God that diverge away from Him till He is out of sight and out of hearing; and because the greatest and best minds in all the Christian centuries have used the highest faculties of reason and investigation till doubt has melted away in the broader illuminations of the Word, I urge with renewed confidence the claim of the one peace-maker between God and men.

Peace to the heart consumed with its fevers, lacerated with its passions, wounded in its deepest sympathies and affections, tainted with the poison of self-love, till touched and pervaded with the love of God. And it is not touched and pervaded with the love of God while He is far off in the eternal abyss; or a sovereign enforcing arbitrary decrees only for his own solitary glory. But through this mediation He does open the channels for our hearts to go up to Him and the Divine heart to throb down to us and fill this great chasm in the soul, this want of some object worthy of its immortal desires and endless aspirations.

Peace to the conscience. What anxiety, what weariness in endless self-analysis, in always looking into ourselves; in trying to take ourselves to pieces and put ourselves together again as they do watches that will not keep time. This is what some people call self-culture, and it is a kind of culture which too much followed is sure to end in self-bewilderments and self-disgusts. How unsatisfying this kind of self-culture, at least to a spiritual nature quick and intuitive! Do your best, and it is not God's best, and the accuser has you in his eye and follows you with equal steps and corners you up and goads and worries you. Acting from ourselves only we do nothing that satisfies us and always carry about the burden of a tormenting self-consciousness. And you rest from this by passing over through the Christ to Him who takes the work upon Himself in the sovereign mouldings of the Divine grace.

Peace after storms; for in the one Mediator are solved those mysteries of life and death that perplex and trouble us. For He turns upon them the light of immortality and shows the end they are working out; and seen thus they are like the crests of the waves when kissed by the breaking sunbeams and sinking into calm. And so for the mind and the heart and the conscience, and for the events that bear us onward, "There is one peace-maker between God and men — the man Christ Jesus."

CHRISTMAS SONG.

CALM on the listening ear of night
    Come heaven's melodious strains,
Where wild Judæa stretches forth
    Her silver mantled plains;
Celestial choirs from courts above
    Shed sacred glories there,
And angels, with their sparkling lyres,
    Make music on the air.

The answering hills of Palestine
    Send back the glad reply,
And greet from all their holy heights
    The Day-Spring from on high;
O'er the blue depths of Galilee,
    There comes a holier calm,
And Sharon waves, in solemn praise,
    Her silent groves of palm.

"Glory to God!" The lofty strain
    The realm of ether fills,
How sweeps the song of solemn joy
    O'er Judah's sacred hills!
"Glory to God!" The sounding skies
    Loud with their anthems ring,
"Peace on the earth; good will to men
    From heaven's Eternal King."

Light on thy hills, Jerusalem!
　The Saviour now is born,
And bright on Bethlehem's joyous plains
　Breaks the first Christmas morn,
And brightly on Moriah's brow
　Crowned with her temple spires,
Which first proclaim the new-born light,
　Clothed with its orient fires.

This day shall Christian tongues be mute,
　And Christian hearts be cold?
Oh, catch the anthem that from heaven
　O'er Judah's mountains rolled,
When burst upon that listening night
　The high and solemn lay:
"Glory to God, on earth be peace,"
　Salvation comes to-day!

III.

THE WILL-POWER.

(A SERMON IN LENT.)

LUKE xxii. 42. *Not my will but thine.*

THE days preceding the crucifixion of Christ were the season during which He walked in the shadow of death. The shadow began to fold Him in as He came down from the Mount of Transfiguration; and soon after commenced his last journey to Jerusalem. The whole twelve are with Him now, and He announces to them plainly that He is going up to be crucified. They fall behind in amazement and fear, for the dread shadow comes over them now for the first time. Gethsemane, however, is the place where the shadow falls thick and heavy. Unbelievers are fond of contrasting the anguish of Jesus at this time with the bravery and firmness with which other martyrs have met the same extremity. They little know through what struggle those other martyrs emerged into the light. It is not merely the shadow of physical death that falls upon Jesus now. The scene in Gethsemane gives us a view of that struggle in its final consummation which takes place in all good men who get the victory, and which is intense and profound in all natures which are themselves profound and great. Small or shallow natures know little or nothing about it. But in great ones there is a descent into the depths of weakness ere there is a rise to the sublimest heights of power. You must look a little farther on if you would see of what all this scene in Gethsemane was the preparation and the prelude. Afterward He says, " All power is given me both in heaven and on the earth." And again, " O fools and slow of heart to believe; ought not Christ to have suffered these things and to enter into his glory?" Weakness, prostration, prone on the earth to the verge of annihilation — this is the scene in Gethsemane. Power described in terms of exaltation and omnipotence — this is the scene forty days afterwards.

These days, when the death-shadow rested upon the Saviour, the older churches observe as the days of Lent, and we are in the midst of them now. In those churches they are days of fasting, in which the usual pleasures of life are postponed, the churches are draped in mourning and dirges are sung in place of anthems. I doubt not that those who observe these rites in good faith, are helped by them and brought into more living sympathy with a suffering Redeemer. What we need supremely is, not sentiment, but such sympathy with Him at the trial hour as will render to us its meaning, so that the same strength shall become ours in the time of need. This is all gathered up and expressed in the prayer — Not as I will, but as thou wilt. It is the absorption of the human will in the Divine, and for this comes down the strengthening angel. For this are all our Lenten days of humiliation, and they do nothing for us except as the prayer goes up out of our weakness and gets its answer. This, however, leads us into the heart of a great subject. There are two phases of character which appear under the full operation of the Gospel upon the human heart. They seem at first inconsistent, antagonistic, and wholly irreconcilable. First, there is weakness, humility, non-resistance, turning both cheeks to the smiter; what seems often to a man of the world pusilanimity and cowardice. The Gospel requires of him who receives it to give up his own will. Hence self-abasement, humiliation, and self-surrender are reckoned among the Christian virtues, and hence the apparent weakness it produces as the lion-heart is tamed and made a lamb.

Then again the Gospel in the person of its believers is mighty and aggressive; and one man clothed in its full power becomes more invincible than an army with banners. Non-resistance, weakness, humiliation disappear, and a single man or a single woman becomes so strong that the forces of an empire may beat against them in vain.

Some have fixed upon one of these phases and some the other, and so from two very opposite stand-points come two classes of objections against the practical value of the Christian faith and confession. These objections are as old as the writers of the second century who assailed the Christian revelation, and they are as new as the disciples of Carlyle who assail it still, in the same way. Unquestionably, it is the blending of these apparent opposites which constitutes the highest human excellence which the Gospel aims to produce. It is Gethsemane alongside of Ascension Mount. It is the complete surrender of our will-power and receiving it back again as no longer ours. The subject expands in a threefold division.

The nature of this will-power;

Its dangers when standing alone;

Its sublime resources when absorbed in the will divine.

I. As to its nature, we shall not get much help from the metaphysicians, but a great deal of light from our common experience. If you take a ball of snow and toss it into the stream, you will witness a rapid disintegration of the mass. It grows less and less till it assimilates to the surrounding substance and disappears. But if you take a piece of quartz, and throw that into the water, you observe that it sinks down to the sandy bottom and lies there. The waves beat over it year after year, and it loses no whit of its integrity, but remains an insoluble element in the waves. So again, plunge one person into the current of human society, and you will see by and by that society draws out of him all that was positive and absorbs it. The stream washes out of him all his individuality, all that was specially his, and dissolves it in the current. His opinions, tastes, sentiments, prejudices, loves, and hates are assimilated and merged in the common mass. Put another person in this same human current, and he never is merged in it, but preserves the same flinty outlines amid all the surgings of the waves. He is himself through all changes, and never disintegrated by the current. Now these contingencies do not depend upon our intellect, culture, or sensibility; upon any amount of personal acquirements and accomplishments. A man may have all these, and yet he may merge them in the current, and they may all play to its motions. It depends altogether upon the amount of WILL which he possesses, whether he is to fall into the stream as a flint or a snow-flake; so that will may be defined as the power of self-cohesion — that which preserves a man's *peculium* amid the flux and reflux of society. A very weak intellect with a very strong will, can preserve a man's selfhood entire and even make it cut like a diamond; and there may be a weak will and an intellect like Milton's; yea, like one of Milton's archangels, and yet it shall lie open to the invasion of every current, and be washed like a feather into the channel.

Will, then, is the power of self-cohesion ; it is the power of resistance to the changes that take place outside of us. This extends even to the body. With some people the human system imbibes disease, as the sponge imbibes water, and they suck in every lurking epidemic from the poisoned air. Others have the power of throwing it off, and it rebounds from them as water does from an oil covering. Dr. Kane was an invalid who travelled for health, and up in the ice regions, with the thermometer at 70° below zero, kept off the cold from the seat of life, while stronger men were yielding to its death-grasp. It is always the will-people — those who have the power of self-cohesion in largest measure, who in these cases are apt to lead a charmed life in the midst of death.

It is.the will that makes a man preëminently what he is. It is the power that sits back of all his other powers and keeps him an integer in the currents and whirls of life. Keep that strong, and all their washings cannot even smooth off the edges of his character. Let that be touched with weakness and he dissolves at once into the elements, and ceases to be an integral force in the universe. And here it is — just here, that the Gospel comes and lays its healthful and healing hand. For if the will is gained, everything else is gained. If that be lost, everything is lost.

II. And this leads us on to the second topic — What are its dangers and perversions when left to itself and standing alone.

Its dangers are twofold. And the first is, that it degenerate into self-will or mere wilfulness, which is one of the worst perversions of the mere natural mind. It is manifest in two ways. It shows itself by sticking upon non-essentials while it leaves out the weightier matters of the law. It will go the whole lengths for the mint, the anise, and the cummin, and even sacrifice unto these justice, mercy, and faith. It would go to the stake merely to have its own way whether right or wrong; and people generally talk the loudest about their consciences when they only mean their self-will. Moreover, when this power degenerates into wilfulness, its demonstrations are always those of passion and self-love, and even on the side of right it attempts to serve the altars of God with the fires of hell. A great many cases of martyrdom which men praise, and which have gone into the calendar of saints, will be found, I think, to be nothing else than sheer wilfulness. No Gethsemane has preceded *their* Calvary; no descent into the deeps of human weakness; and therefore they rise no higher than mere bravery, wilful endurance, stoical obstinacy, and dramatic virtue; not to the sublime heights where they reappear in the clothings of Divine Omnipotence.

But a worse danger than that besets this power

when standing alone, and that is that it be broken down and destroyed. Oh, there is no sadder spectacle in this world than that of a man whose will has been broken down; who sees the right, who desires to follow it, and yet when he tries to do it finds himself weaker than an infant at the breast. The intellect may be clear, and the sensibilities may be alive, and there may be all the accomplishments and adorning graces of the outward man, and all the ties of friendship may be twined about him, and all the motives of heaven and hell may lie upon him, and yet *some demon has touched the will and broken it*, and it is as if the mainspring had been taken out and all the wheels go whirring at random. There is no longer any self-cohesion for that man. He is at the mercy of every temptation that comes, and "his limed soul when struggling to be free is more engaged." " I have a large fortune," said a man to a temperance agent, " but tell me how I can pass that dram-shop without going in and I will give you the whole of it." And here is where sin does its deadliest mischief, and herein lies all the bondage of evil habit. Every repetition of the sin makes the will weaker, till finally its power of volition is gone forever.

There was once a man whose intellect was burnished to a most unwonted brightness, as fervid a genius as our American culture ever evolved. But he gave himself to the tempter once and again, and before he knew it this awful power of will was drawn clean out of him, and he fell and lay prone; and then no strengthening angel could lift him up, for there was nothing to take hold of. He fell, and the knell that sounded over him was like his own song of the bells : —

> "Iron bells!
> Every sound that floats
> From the rust within their throats
> Is a groan."

But I need not have gone so far, nor have recited an extreme case like this. The reason everywhere why virtue is so feeble is because the will is weak and wayward. All that class of persons that halt between Christ and the world, and do not know to whom they belong themselves, are people whose wills have been demagnetized and hence all their weakness and inefficiency. There is no decision in religion where this is the case, no self-consecration to duty, but a passive floating along as circumstance or accident or pleasure may direct the way. They are creatures of accident or creatures of society, for the sole reason that the will is weak; for when the will is weak the world has us in its power, and a full grown manhood or womanhood is an impossible attainment.

III. All the dangers I have described we avoid when the human will is merged and lost in the Divine. Two things are essential to this, the surrender of all things, and receiving them back again as no longer ours. The former is the hardest thing the Christian has to do. It is the Gethsemane through which he passes on his way to Mount Ascension. It is the real Lenten season, and unless his forty days' fastings betoken this, they are nothing but dietary rules, and will be followed by no Easter morning. I fear there is not much of this giving up without some secret reservations. These secret reservations are the source of all your halting and weakness. One person has some indolent habit to indulge, another has gains accumulating by sinful traffic or by putting things the best side out; another has wordly vanities to support, and so charity and mercy must beg and starve; another has the blandishments of private friendship which would be perilled by a whole confession and consecration; another has his patrons to please, and the popular will which he must court and follow after; another dreads the danger of non-conformity with the scribes and pharisees; another lives only in the senses, and can see nothing to live for but animal enjoyments, and no soul in himself or any one else to be cared for and saved; and so these persons do not cast themselves without reserve upon the eternal and all-perfect law. But when my opinions, my pleasures, my gains, my righteousness, and all that makes up my personality as a responsible being, are brought in entire surrender to the

Divine will and then received back again, a higher will than mine sways me henceforth, as the current sways the lily on its bosom. To make us do this the whole plan of Providence is arranged. It is to break down wilfulness, that the Divine will-power may take its place, and to this end sometimes He smites us blow after blow, before He can crush it down. Sometimes it takes years to break it, and sometimes like an anvil it grows harder under the strokes. Very often the spirit is broken when the will is not given up at all. Very often, too, the will is weakly given up to a fellow mortal, but no whit of it surrendered to God. Very often it yields to the tempter when it will not yield to the Lord, and becomes weak as a palsied limb. But when it does yield to Him, perfectly, and without any reserve, another will is received in its place. It is not mine, and I know in my deepest consciousness that it is God moved into the soul, and seeking to be realized in all my speech and actions. There it is always present, and I can feel its motions and its thrills of pleasure or of pain. The Christian who has once given up all things and received them back, has an experience answering somewhat to that of the Master himself. "All thine are mine, and mine are thine, and thou art glorified in them." Two things immediately follow. First, wilfulness, which is but a poor aping of conscientiousness, immediately disappears. In things merely personal and non-essential, we can be as pliant and yielding as a little child. And here comes in the full scope and exercise of all that class of virtues which worldly men sometimes mistake for pusillanimity,— meekness, gentleness, deference, and the sweet charities and amenities of life. These come as the manifestations of the Divine within us, just as his great power around us runs down into the smallest channels, and hangs leaves and blossoms on the smallest stems, and threads them with pencillings finer than the artist can copy.

Hence the contradictions of the Christian character are apparent and not real. Under the most of yielding and gentleness and many-sidedness, which the Apostle describes as "all things to all men," the will-determinations may be the strongest and most absolute. Wilfulness runs into obstinacy on things indifferent. The will, absorbed in the Divine, can yield as God yields, bending to occasions and changes with myriad-minded goodness, because there is an unchanging purpose within the whole. From our reception of the Divine will we bend with gentle adaptations to the peace, the comfort, and even the whims and caprices of our fellows, so far as the unchanging purpose is not hurt nor compromised. But within the non-essential and in things that pertain to justice, mercy, and essential truth, we are made strong in God's Omnipotence. God is omnipotent in and through us, for his will is done on earth as it is in heaven. Hence the Gospel contrasts. In the depths of humiliation, " Not my will but thine ; " in the heights of exaltation, " All power is given me in heaven and on the earth."

There is only one remedy for those whose will is wayward or whose power of virtue is broken down. Outward props will not avail. Legal restraints and prudential motives will not avail. These have been tried again and again, and in such cases always in vain. There is no human help when the awful power of will has been undermined, except as human help may be a guide to something higher than itself. But there is Divine help, and out of it on men once lying prone and helpless have been wrought the greatest miracles on record. Augustine was gone clean down in vice when God laid hold of him and lifted him up and put a new will into him, and he stands like a peak of granite for the centuries to date from. So the weakest will of the most wayward among you, if you would give it up to Him without reservations, would be returned to you infrangible as adamant. But to gain this you must go down with Jesus into the shades of Gethsemane, and watch with Him and suffer with Him where self lies prone and bleeding, till its surrender is complete and the angel's face beams through the shadows from above. And then the shadows of the Lenten days are fringed already with the Ascension glories.

PEACE, BE STILL.

'T is not, my God, thy chastening hand,
  'T is not the pain I bear,
That hangs upon my drooping heart
  This heavy load of care.

But myriads move on wingèd feet
  Made swift to do thy will,
While thy dread silence on me falls,
  Thy mandate — Peace, be still.

All Nature's harps, in endless ranks,
  By thy sweet breath are stirred;
And through my prison windows float
  The sounds of breeze and bird.

Then up and up through golden air,
  Beyond Time's ebb and flow,
I see the throngs, who cast their crowns,
  In white robes bending low.

They come and go on flashing wings,
  For all thine errands fleet;
While here, thy hand is on my lips,
  Thy chains are on my feet.

Thus from my bed of chronic pain
  I prayed — "O Lord, how long!"

Pining to reap the harvest fields
And sing the harvest song.

And in the hush of silence falls
This answer to my prayer, —
"What gave those throngs their flashing wings,
Whence come the robes they wear?

"Ere yet by word or deed or song
Made swift to do my will,
They learned it in the trial-hour
Beneath my — Peace, be still!

"And He who walked the garden shades
The best beloved Son,
Prayed, ere the strengthening angel came —
'Thy will, not mine, be done!'"

IV.

CALVARY.

(GOOD FRIDAY.)

JOHN XII. 32. *And I, if I be lifted up from the earth, will draw all men unto me. This He said, signifying what death He should die.*

THE fundamental facts on which the whole Christian system rests are ranged into a series; each one of which necessitates all the rest. The birth of Christ, his mission, his miracles, his death, his resurrection, his ascension, his coming again as the Paraclete, will be found so connected in the narratives of the New Testament that you cannot take out one without impairing the significance of all. For example, if you regard his death as the death of any other man, or of a common martyr, his resurrection becomes less credible and significant; and all that strain of prophecy which runs through his teachings, forecasting his death and resurrection as included in a great plan of human salvation, has no meaning at all. Hence when one of the facts of this divine series has been expunged, the rest are pretty sure to follow in logical order, until Christianity is reduced to a mere system of natural religion. If

Jesus was born as other men, why should He not die as other men; and if He died as other men, why should not his resurrection be like that of other men, and why should He come again as Spirit and Comforter? But let all these facts be retained and their relation to each other studied and pondered, and it is not long before a system of divine truth rises on our faith, flinging its light over the mysteries of two worlds and lighting up the darkness of the grave.

You know how much meaning in the New Testament gathers and centres about the cross of Christ. His death is made a moral and spiritual necessity in the Providence of God. He is the Lamb slain from the foundation of the world. Hence all through his ministry Jesus speaks of "his hour." His enemies were powerless to touch his life till *his hour* had come. And when his hour was come He says, "For this was I born and for this cause came I into the world." And again, "If I be lifted up, I will draw all men unto me."

In unfolding so great a subject as the *significance of the cross of Christ*, we must not fall into the error of making it sole and exclusive; as if the whole work of redemption were concentrated here. In that way we should fling disparagement on the other facts of the Gospel history. On the other hand, if we may enter aright into the meaning of this great sacrifice, all those other facts will be seen in the light of it, and the whole system of Christian faith appear in new consistency and beauty.

I. First, then, we say, that the cross is an expression out of profounder depths of the Divine Love than the world had ever known before or since. The Jew only saw God apart and alone in his awful justice. He only knew God set over against man in fearful antagonism, — God in his dazzling holiness, man in his sin and his uncleanness liable to be invaded with avenging thunders. No human wit would have imagined the way in which this fearful gulf was to be bridged over. The idea of the Divine coming over to us — taking upon itself our human burdens of sin and suffering — would have entered into no *human* scheme of reconciliation. And yet this is the great truth daily brought home to us in the cross of Christ. It need not be embarrassed by any subtile questions about the union of the Father and the Son. "God so loved the world that He gave his only begotten Son;" and "He was in Him reconciling the world unto Himself." The Divine Justice in the Christian Gospel becomes simply the form and aspect of the Divine Goodness, moulding it and keeping it from missing its mark. Sacrifice means the giving of one's self away for the good of others, and the sacrifice of Christ is called "complete" because nothing was kept back, and it is doubly significant because the love of the Father is imaged and shown forth in the sacrifice of the Son. The Son does not come to ward off the Father's wrath or deflect his thunderbolts, but to make new channels through which the Father's love could find its way to the hearts of men. It is the Divine Love, therefore, coming into the world anew through the only begotten Son, — love which delights to give itself away, stops at no suffering, but sends out nerves into every one's condition and draws up a world's agony into its own heart. Hence while it is capable of the heights of rapture it is capable also of the infinite depths of sorrow. The Divine Compassion as revealed in Jesus becomes altogether personal, and if He incarnates and represents the Divine nature as He claims to do, then the Father is not an awfully impassive Being away off beyond the stars, but a present Redeemer bearing our griefs and sorrows on his tenderest feeling every hour. You have looked, I presume, on a group of statuary which represents a wife kneeling over the form of her dead soldier, her countenance raised in strange blendings of raptured devotion and broken-hearted anguish, all expressed in the prayer, "O God I give him to his country and to thee." These images of finite human affection will give us some conception of what it was for the Father to give his only begotten Son, and they will make it very easy to understand why the sorrow folded in the shadows of Gethsemane appears unlike the sufferings of commom martyrdom, because it gives us gleams of an infinite compassion which has taken on its feeling the sins and sufferings of a race.

What a scheme of salvation *we* should have planned out, as fitted for an Almighty Being to adopt! We should have called Him down from heaven, probably on the car of his Omnipotence, slaying the wicked, and taking up the saints into Paradise. That was the Messiah which men looked for, and which some look for yet. And yet He came concealing his glory, holding in his power, sinking himself in our condition, hiding himself under our poverty and wretchedness out of tender regard for our moral freedom, so as to win his way into the soul by the most of love and the least of fear. So then the cross on Calvary shows what a cross there was in the Divine Love, which consented to hide its power but to halve the anguish, in order to find our fallen humanity and lift it up to the Divine Embrace.

II. There is all this in the cross of Christ, and of consequence there is another truth which it holds aloft, and which it preaches every day to the world. It is the depth and the malignity of human sinfulness. There is only one step in the argument which shows how vast is the moral ruin which requires such a reconstruction as this. If you say sin is only a superficial matter — only a wrinkling of the rind and not a disease that lies at the core — you will easily think that God would not be at much pains about it. He would let it alone, and let it work itself off in the natural unfoldings of our manhood, just as the bark peels off in the growth of the tree. And then to accommodate all things to such a conception, you will discharge Christianity of all its supernatural meaning. The blood of the covenant is a common thing, and the death of Christ is the death of a common man. And then those words, Selfishness, and Hate, and Pride, and Revenge, and Lust, and Cruelty, and love of Rule, which enter into the idea of sin, and make it up, will not express to you evils that take hold of the immortal nature and blight it. They only mar it a little on the outside, will pass off with a little more development, and without repentance or humiliation. Restore the Gospel to its integrity and its full orbed power, and how vastly different do all these things appear! Let the incarnation be indeed the Word made flesh; the death on Calvary not the untimely end of a defeated Jewish Reformer, but the Lamb slain from the foundation of the world, and then the question comes home at once, What eternal interests were at stake, requiring such a descent of the Divine Love into the depths of our human woe? We shall easily see that it was no speck on the surface of humanity, but a plague-spot at the heart, that was to be removed. Would all this costly sacrifice be made — this gift of the Son of God to go down into the profound of sorrow and suffering — merely for the removal of some superficial evil, which the race would outgrow of itself, and not rather of one that lay at the Heart, like a canker, and threatened ruin to the whole? Not alone then the depths of the Divine Love for man, but the depths of the Divine Hate towards sin — the only thing that perils his eternal peace, is shadowed forth on Calvary, and makes us cease to wonder almost at the darkness that came down and involved the sacrifice.

There is something which delights the imagination in the ministry of angels. Through the old dispensation they led on the chosen people, and in all ages of the world such ministries have inspired its childlike faith. So they might have come, never putting on our garments of mortality; beckoning to the skies, but never touching the earth themselves to be soiled by it. So it might have been, if men only needed teaching and beckoning upward. But there was One who came down into our condition, wrapped the garments of our infancy and manhood about Him that He might be put in communion therewith and thrill them with life and energy; and He becomes not teacher only, but Redeemer; not a guide merely to beckon, but a Saviour to quicken and regenerate; and so when St. John draws the veil and gives us gleams of the ritual of heaven, it is of one who has helped us by sharing our whole human experience that He might adapt the Divine

Help to it, and to whom worship is always rendered under the symbol of suffering and sacrifice.

It is a doctrine, you know, of some branches of the modern Church, that God himself in the person of Christ, suffered as a substitute for man, and so his death becomes the sole condition of forgiveness. Do not denounce the doctrine till you first eliminate what is false from it, and then take home the truth; for it has melted the iron out of many a sinful soul, and given it peace in believing. It is not the supposed commercial transfer of our sins to Christ, and his merits to us that gives the peace. It is the thought that Christ represents here the infinite Mercy; that God himself can come over to us, and make our case his own; that He so hates the evil that spreads canker through the tenderest places of the heart, that He will take the burden of it upon himself; that He will let our hardness and impenitence put stabs into his wounded love before He will let us go; that not his Fatherhood alone, on the peaks of heaven, but his humanity, brought nigh and inserted in our lowly condition, is given in sacrifice for us every hour; it is this that will make you hate your sin, if anything will, and let the heart melt in repentance, and the Divine Grace clear its stains out of you in showers of effacing rain.

III. Again we look to the cross of Christ to get some just estimate of the worth and grandeur of human nature. We are very apt to fall into mere declamation on this head. The greatness of human nature implies a twofold capacity — susceptibilities for progress and enjoyment, and susceptibilities for degradation and suffering. The possible heights of its exaltation measure the possible depths of its downfall. Natures that are small and narrow and low down, have these susceptibilities in slight degree. They can neither rise nor sink very far. But all those provisions for human salvation which we call supernatural, are so many testimonies to the endless value of the human soul. You begin to see the worth of a thing when you see how much it costs to buy it or redeem it. Seeing only the surface of men, liable only to physical evils and physical death, all the supernatural agencies of the New Testament are utterly incredible. Would God come into the world in this wise, giving over such a Being as Jesus Christ to the agonies of the cross, to save an insect of to-day from a little more or a little less of physical evil? How great are the means and how insignificant is the end! How costly the price and how poor in comparison is the thing purchased! But the cross proclaims forever that physical suffering, even in the person of God's only Son, is to be reckoned of less account, where a spiritual and eternal good can be achieved by it. Expunge the supernatural from Christianity, make its Christ a common man, and his cross a human misfortune, and we tend by inevitable logic to that view of human nature which merges it in mere animal existence. But the moment we understand that man neither enjoys nor suffers like an animal, that the pleasures and pains of sense are hardly worthy of a moment's thought, compared with those pleasures or pains that are to fill up the measure of its capacities forever; the moment we understand all this, the grand array of means provided in the Christian Gospel to lift man up and save him become the logical necessities of the Divine Providence. The mystery of the cross clears away, and the Great Sacrifice is no waste of treasure and blood. We wonder not that the heavens should bend down to the earth, and break into its affairs, when we see that this world with all its trappings could not be given in exchange for a human soul. So the cross preaches to us the love of God as a personal love; the depth of ruin into which man is plunged by sin; and the worth and grandeur of human nature in its unmeasured capacities for rising or falling, for bliss or for suffering.

IV. But there is another truth which comes home to us as preached by the cross of Christ. It clears away the mystery of death, for it shows death as the reverse side of resurrection. Death, as we learn it here, is not an isolated fact in human experience, and resurrection another isolated fact. Death is only the hither side of one great fact — the waning of our mortal being, that the immortal being may have freedom and enlargement. This waxes as the other wanes. How conspicuous is the fact in the last days of our Saviour's earthly life! More and more does the mortal body appear as the mere foliage of the Divine and immortal being, the foliage lit up with wondrous transfigurations from the Divine man within who could not be touched by the spear and the nails. On the very eve of crucifixion — speaking out of this divine consciousness — we are told, "In that hour Jesus rejoiced in spirit and said, Now is the Son of Man glorified, and God is glorified in Him." That has always seemed to me an instance of the highest moral sublime. The cross, just before, but the way to "the glorification of the Son of Man." And what a light from this Exemplar is flung over all our death-scenes and Gethsemanes, which have been so multiplied of late and sent sorrow and anguish into so many homes! Ties must break and hearts must bleed and death will come by sudden violence until men grow wiser and better. At the same time let the light that streams from the cross be turned full upon our vales of sorrow and our Calvaries of suffering, and we shall remember that death is only the hither side of resurrection unto life, and that the darkest midnights are broken by the dawn of the Easter mornings.

Men pass in long processions, sometimes in agonized groups and companies, into the freezing shadows of night; and how many a heart to-day is broken and bleeding because its treasures have been snatched away by sudden havoc and ruin.[1] The cross is the symbol which hangs aloft over all the wrecks of our slaughtered humanity; the symbol of a love which drew all that havoc and agony up into its own experience, in order to show it the reverse side of resurrection and immortality. Our human mortality is the cloud which hangs between us and the glory just beyond; the cloud thick and heavy until the Christ turned it into white wreaths which only temper to our condition the ardent mercies of the Lord. Such is the fourfold meaning of the cross and such the light streaming from it to-day.

There is one point of application which the subject urges upon you. It rebukes our sleepy indifference and dull consciousness of the powers that slumber within us. Would that we might see the worth of human nature as God sees it who has expended so much to cleanse and save it. If we considered the vast possibilities for good or evil, for sorrow or joy, which are wrapped up within us and are slumbering there; there could be no such thing as religious insensibility. We should be awake to the mighty issues of this probation now and here. It is quite conceivable that when these capacities

[1] This sermon was preached soon after one of the most fatal steamboat disasters.

are all developed and filled up, having cast off the coverings and clogs of earth, an hour of suffering will outweigh all its physical pains, and an hour of joy all its earth-born pleasures. And the Son of Man is lifted up not by his death alone, yea rather through that by his resurrection and coming again in Spirit that He may draw you to himself. For not by the cross is He lifted up as an object for our pitying gaze, but by this He is raised above all the centuries to his place of power, that our gaze upon Him by an act of faith may bring healing and cleansing mercy.

THE TWISTED THORN.

Night hath shut the prisoner in,
Night of terror, night of sin;
Vain for light my eyeballs roll,
Darkly here I dwell in dole;
On my couch I plain and mourn,
Bleeding with the twisted thorn.

What arises dark and still?
Oh, 't is Calvary's awful hill!
Lo, the drooping sufferer there!
Lo, the unprevailing prayer!
Lo, the temples pierced and torn,
Bleeding with the twisted thorn!

What arises clear and still?
'T is Ascension's sacred hill!
See the rifted clouds retire,
Flaming with the fleecy fire,
Through them see a form upborne —
He who wore the twisted thorn!

What is that I see afar?
'T is the blinking of a star;
'T is Orion! 'tis the Sun!
'T is the Conqueror coming on,
Riding through the gates of Morn,
He who wore the twisted thorn.

Look ye up to Calvary's hill,
Ye who bear the pains of ill;
Look ye towards Ascension Mount,
Ye who drink the bitter fount;
Look ye towards the gates of Morn,
Ye who wear the twisted thorn!

V.

RESURRECTION AND ASCENSION.

(EASTER.)

ACTS i. 9. *While they beheld, He was taken up; and a cloud received Him out of their sight.*

LUKE, beyond all reasonable question, is the author of the book of Acts, and he reports the scene of our Saviour's ascension evidently from the testimony of eye-witnesses. The scene as described could not have been on the earth but beyond the bourne of mortality. It was in the spirit-world, of which for the time these disciples had open cognizance; but that ceasing, "a cloud"—this cloud of mortality—hung between them and the risen Saviour. The "two men in white apparel," or the angels who appear upon the scene, assure the astonished disciples that they will see Jesus come again *in like manner* as they have seen Him go away. *How* He went away some of the disciples seem not to have understood, and so they mistook the manner of his coming again. It is not the first instance in which the high utterances which have come down out of heaven have been taken in a lower and grosser sense than that in which they were made. From these and similar declarations made by our Lord himself pertaining to his second coming, probably the notion originated among the early disciples, of a second coming of Christ upon the earth through the clouds of the air.

What are we to understand by the ascension of Christ? Simply and only his resurrection consummated and complete. It cannot be necessary to argue with any rational mind, that the New Testament writers do not mean an ascent through space into the sky. They mean that having put off all the remnants of mortality which clung to Him from the tomb, He ascended into the sphere of celestial and divine being which mortal eyes cannot look upon, and so *in the flesh* they saw Him no more. Henceforth He will appear out of heaven only in like manner as they saw Him go into it.

The death and ascension, or complete resurrection, of Christ are the two facts which mainly occupy our attention as we contemplate the closing scenes in the life of Jesus. One is the human and finite, the other is the divine side of that wondrous life. We are apt to get a very narrow view of these two facts that very much tames down their significance. By the death of Christ is not meant merely his expiration on Calvary. By the resurrection and ascension are not meant merely the reanimation of the corpse in Joseph's tomb, much less going up into the air from

Ascension Mount. By no means. Bear in mind that there was in Him the union of our tempted, suffering, dying humanity, with the all-revealing and indwelling divinity. At first the suffering human nature is dominant and conspicuous. He is a man of sorrows; He hath not where to lay his head; He bends under the weight of temptation that lies against Him with its terrible load. But within all this the divinity gleams, at first faintly, then more openly, then with transfiguring power and splendor. This waxes and the other wanes. At length the mortal suffering nature is expelled and the divine man rises clear of it into his tranquil and unclouded noon. In the first stages a man of sorrows and acquainted with grief. In the last stage is the triumphal strain, "All power is given me in heaven and upon the earth."

Now we observe that the first process — the passing away of the encumbering and suffering humanity, is called our Lord's death. The other and the reverse process, the emergence out of it of the half-concealed Divinity to its meridian power, is called the Lord's ascension. One kept time with the other. That was a daily death as a means of daily rising, till there was nothing left to be excluded, and the whole Divine man ascends before us and above us as the image of the invisible God.

That I do not give too broad a rendering to these two inverse terms of the Gospel you will be abundantly satisfied if you examine and collate the passages where they occur. They are given always as the exact image of our own spiritual progress and enlargement. We rise and ascend with Him only as we die with Him. The self-denials and the conflicts which He calls taking up the cross daily, the temptation scenes, the Gethsemanes and the Calvarys alike ; these are included under this term, dying with Christ. And then the lower, the tempted nature, wanes till it disappears, and the angel-power from within unfolds and ascends free of it ; and this is rising with Christ.

And you will see, I think, at once why the ascension of Christ is the fact which lies at the very heart of the Gospel and is the hiding-place of its power. For it was only by his ascension that He came spiritually to his Church and comes to it now in showers of grace and love. And you will see the poverty and meagreness of the theologies which gather up the chief meaning of our Saviour's mission in those six hours of physical suffering. Not so Paul. " If Christ be not *risen* your faith is vain, ye are yet in your sins." And he announces himself a witness of this rising. But how a witness ? He never saw Christ in the flesh that we know of. He was not at the tomb that great Sabbath morning. He met Christ for the first time, on his way to Damascus, breaking upon him out of the glories of the Syrian sky. Such being the broad significance of these two leading facts of the Gospel history, let us now proceed to turn the light of the great truth which is here involved upon our own lowly and suffering state. For the great Exemplar is placed before us to fling illustration over all our mortal condition. Standing on Mount Ascension we shall see revealed more clearly the hopes of man and the possibilities that sleep within us. If we are planted together in the likeness of his death we shall be also in the likeness of his resurrection. Death and ascension! These two are the leading facts of the Christian probation and experience as we follow the divine footsteps. There is not in us the same "fullness of the Godhead" which Christ had, but there is in us the heavenly man clogged and concealed under the earthly, and one waxes as the other wanes.

I. See this first in our most external changes. You observe that there is nothing fixed here, and that even our houses and homes are but as tents which are pitched for a day and a night upon the plain. Now you will find generally that even this economy of temporal change is necessitated by deeper changes and growths within us. We build our habitations; we gather our families about us as the nestling places of our affections; nay, even the stones and the trees and the shrubbery have grown into us and become almost a part of our being, for the heart's tendrils have gone out and laid their clasp upon them all. It seemed at first that we were to stay there in one place forever. But we find at length we had exhausted all it had to give us as a means of life's work, discipline and duty. There is a growing maladjustment of what is around us to what is within us. We must gird up ourselves and rend off the fastenings of the heart, and the former things must pass away. So it is when the young man shuts off the scene of his boyhood, its fields, brooks, orchards, and groves, for a new plunge into the world. So it is when the young woman foregoes the ties of girlhood for a new and more sacred vow. The spot where we had taken root, where we had loved with our young loves and dreamed our waking dreams, and where we were held by all the twinings of the heart, has exhausted its resources upon us. We must pluck up the roots of our old life and turn away from its scenery forever. So it is all through this world with its enlarging responsibilities. We must forego the past, ofttimes with ties that bleed where they break, but exscinding the old is the stern condition of our enlargement. We may remain where we are and let the moss and the mould gather upon us; but if we would avoid all this we must rend the heart's claspings from loved and familiar things and let them go out again. Our very surroundings as we pass out of them become the sheddings of the soul. Our most external life then gives us this image of our death to the old, and ascension out of it.

But changes more inward and spiritual are also represented. The regeneration of the individual finds its perfect image in the resurrection and ascension of Christ. Perhaps we commence our Christian course with the persuasion that all is smooth and even, that human nature is only to be unfolded like a flower, that development is all we need. The child is born perfectly pure, we thought, and needs only to grow in stature and grow in grace. We very soon find out our mistake. We very soon find that there is an old carnal man to be put off before the angel can be unfolded from within. There is lust and covetousness and bad temper, and a whole brood of hereditary evils that must be resisted and slain, before the heavenly life comes into the consciousness, long before it unfolds with perfect clearness.

We have come to use the word habits to describe the garments that we wear. It describes better the investiture of our souls. Habits are simply petrified loves. We love a certain mode of living. We get used to it and cannot get out of its ruts and grooves. We love certain pleasures and gratifications; we come to depend upon them and cannot do without them. We love ease. It settles down into a fixed habit of indolence, and we cannot without great effort break away from our old sleepy rounds of thought and practice. In this way a great many persons before life is half through get ironed into one set of opinions, usages, and customs; habits of speech, of thought, and of living. And that is the way that this world gets hold of them with grappling hooks and makes them grow old before their time. Old age is simply the external man, both the body and the outward mind growing stiff and hard and shutting in the soul under the iron clamps of custom. Some people get ironed in at thirty, most at forty; and unless Christ has touched their souls, at fifty they are clean gone in religious indifference or theologic petrefactions. Sometimes these people are converted to Christ. But it is by revolution not by growth in grace; the Divine Power coming within with so much violence that the outward natural man is shivered in pieces.

But a Christian life, orderly and heavenly, is a perpetual warfare against these creeping layers of worldliness and evil custom that the life within may uplift them and be kept in everlasting freshness and youth. "If we have been planted together in the likeness of His death we shall be also in the likeness of His resurrection." It is a life of daily denials and renunciations, that the spirit of Christ may flow into them and fill them out with himself. How beautiful is such a life: old things always passing away, the old crumbling Adam constantly put off and the angel taking its place! Thus those who follow the Lord Jesus like little children are always renewing their youth and putting on the beauty of their prime. It is daily death in order to a daily resurrection. It is rising from the dead every hour and walking in newness of life. It is following Him in the regeneration, that as the finite and tempted humanity waned and disappeared till the Divine Man broke unclouded upon the world, so our selfish nature becomes weaker till it dies, and the strong angel disencumbered walks free of it in the likeness of the Lord's resurrection, and rejoices in the blessed Easter days of renewal and glory.

All human progress looks to Christ as its image and representation. The progress of the race is not a continuous ascent, but a decay and a resurrection. When Christ appeared the race was apparently in ruins. Christianity was not a progress, but an emergence out of death and the tomb. It was the uplifting and heaving off of whole ages of effete religion, vast piles of superstition and of dead letter, and a Divine form of religion coming forth in its place. The death and resurrection of Christ become the perfect type of the decay and renovation of the humanity which He assumed and which He came to save. The race is a collective man and passes through the stages of growth and decay. The eastern mythologies are the dead letter of what once was a living religion. The beautiful mythology of Greece is the darkened symbol it may be of a primitive revelation to man. In every form of civilization — Greek, Roman, Egyptian, or Oriental, we have the history of a rise, decline, and fall. Christianity is simply a putting off of the old body and death robes that the new body may emerge out of them. Thus the Christ emerging with conquering strength out of the finite and the earthly, one waxing as the other waned, is a divine picture of all humanity, decaying and ascending out of decay till the redemption of the race on earth becomes complete and the prophecy is fulfilled, — " Behold I create all things new ! "

But the subject has an application which affects us individually and vitally. Over the whole field of natural death a light comes down from Ascension Mount; for there is openly disclosed to us all that is concealed under the vesture of mortal decay. It is solemn, but hardly mysterious when saintly old age passes on; and if the generations went in unbroken ranks death would cast no shadow that would trouble us, the cloud on the thither side would be so completely illumined. When our faculties begin to fold in we begin to die to this world. Gently they are folded in sometimes one after another; sense, and memory, and reason, and at last consciousness — the book of life all closed and sealed and laid away, its contents to outward appearance blurred or blotted out. But they are not blotted out. They are folded in to be kept more securely, and to be opened again leaf after leaf that they may have a resetting and embodiment where decay and death have no longer any control. Thus growing old is a preparation for growing young again ; yea, age only touches the outward man that the man within, more orderly and securely, may have a clear unfolding and ascension and reinvestiture on a field of endless progress and enlargement. But whether old or young, God never calls away his servants till there is a vacant place elsewhere for them to fill; and when the physical life is subordinated to the moral and spiritual, how small is the difference whether the soul's release from it be in age or in youth or in the strength of manhood! Ever and everywhere the life that is pure and heavenly is the surrender of that which is lower to the call and the needs of that which is higher; of that which is outer and more transient to that which is essential and eternal.

These truths come home to us with special power to-day after a period of great sacrifice, in which the Beauty of our Israel has been slain in its high places, and we turn the light from Ascension Mount on the Golgothas of the battle-field. Some of rare gifts and power for good, of our own denomination, and from among yourselves, have joined the long procession of martyrs. They have followed in the path of the Great Sacrifice for humanity. Let us look well to it, that we be found in this great procession; for living or dying, life truly consecrated is a sacrifice and offering unto God. What a privilege, to march in this procession in which prophets and martyrs and noble men and women have walked, and are walking now, at the head of whom is the Christ, breathing his life through all and bidding our step keep time with his! And how animating the thought, that as the heavens fill up and bend over us the more freely and vitally their life and spirit pass into our human affairs and make our lowly service divine. Before we reach the meridian of our life's little day, those who started together have parted company and most of them are on the other side. Young men and women, matrons who had watched and worked with us, strong men who bore the heat and burden of the day, have failed from earth, though not from the grand company yet strong and active to do the divine will. "We do not wish them back again," you say, but you say it mechanically; for the lips say it, not the heart. We do wish them back for earth needs all their activities and energies, and hearts that have once beat together cannot be sundered without the sense of heart-breaking and of baffled sympathies and affections which yearn for the same unison again. And these affections are mightily prophetic; for a voice from them comes out of the very deeps of human nature, assuring us that the veil of mortality is too thin and unsubstantial to keep those apart who are spiritually one in the grand aims and purposes of existence, and in doing the will of Him who unites all his disciples in one great organism, as living branches of a living Vine. While we are trying to give them up they are coming again already, not in visible manifestation but in that tide of spiritual life more full and deep that beats through our heart of hearts from the sphere of immortality. We do not wish them back again? I wish them all back again ; and I doubt not they come back in methods higher than we conceive of or know how to pray for, as they make the heavens more full and strong and make them bend near us and touch us with a more tender and pervading love.

A SONG OF VICTORY.

Sing we now a song of triumph ;
  Leave betimes the shadowy vales
Where the winds across our lute-strings
  Sink to low and sorrowing wails.
Stand we now upon the mountains
  Where the glory shines complete ;
Where the thunders roll beneath us
  Making music at our feet.

Lo, the pathway lies behind us,
  Where we marched o'er heaps of slain :
And our vanquished foes lie bleeding
  All along the battle-plain ; —
All the sordid troop of Mammon ;
  Coward Fear and lust of Praise ;
Death that cast his baleful shadow
  Over all our darkling ways ;

Unbelief that feeds on ashes ;
  Fear of man that brings a snare ;
Selfish Grief and selfish Pleasure ;
  Carnal Pride and haggard Care ;
Satan in fair form transfigured
  Strewing garlands on the road
To install our vaunting Reason
  On the eternal throne of God.

See his rabble host retreating !
Shattered spear and broken shield ;
See his waning camp-fires flicker
All along the conquered field ;
And o'er all like flashing sunbeams
   Waves the mighty Conqueror's sword—
Louder than your Io Pæans
Allelujahs to the Lord !

Then beyond the Silent River
   See the mystic mountains rise !
Range on range away ascending
   Till they kiss the vaulted skies ;
And along their sun-smit summits
   Thousands walk with sparkling feet,
And give back our song of triumph
   In the distance soft and sweet.

From the myriad gleaming turrets
   Whence the billowy music swells,
Clear across the Silent River,
   Float the chimes of morning bells:
They have conquered — we have conquered —
   And one note of triumph raise,
Heaven and earth here join together
   In their grandest song of praise.

Ah ! adown the valley yonder,
   Bending earthward, draped with woe,
Keeping step to funeral dirges,
   Who are they that creep so slow ?
Haste ye swiftly with the tidings
   Wafted from the peaks of day ;
Lead them up to Mount Ascension,
   Fling their scrannel pipes away.

A SONG OF VICTORY.

Give them beauty now for ashes;
  Out of weakness make them strong;
And in place of churchyard music,
  Give the resurrection song,
Which the beauteous lips of loved ones
  That they kissed with sad farewells,
Sing to them from o'er the River
  Mid the chimes of morning bells.

Now the noontide floods the waters,
  Still beneath the silent oar,
And their mocky depths of crystal
  Copy down the immortal shore.
Sing we then upon the mountains
  Where the glory shines complete,
To the conquering Christ hosannas —
  Fling your garlands at his feet!

VI.

INTERCESSIONS OF THE SPIRIT.

(WHITSUNDAY.)

ROMANS viii. 26. *We know not what we should pray for as we ought: but the Spirit itself maketh intercession for us with groanings which cannot be uttered.*

YOU might infer at first from this word "groanings" that the Apostle makes effectual prayer to consist in what are called agonizings, or importunity; as if God were like some fickle parents who deny their children what they simply ask for, but grant it afterwards to their vociferous cries. No such doctrine of prayer is here set forth; and though this word "groanings" sometimes renders the Greek term well enough, it certainly is not the proper word here. More often the word sighing, or deep breathing, is the appropriate rendering.

Looking back a little through the context, you observe that the Apostle describes our weak and suffering nature girded with frailty and mortality and sighing for its deliverance. He sees the whole creation travailing in pain. Not only those whom the Gospel has not enlightened and blessed, but those also who have the first-fruits of the Spirit, into whom the promised Comforter has descended, have the same travailings and sighings for redemption. And here the Apostle interposes in the text his doctrine of encouragement and consolation. We are not groping in the dark. These sighings of the world are not the private praying of individuals. They are the Spirit of God that intercedes and prophesies within us. They are the Divine voice that issues out of depths profounder than our own weaknesses and infirmities, rising straight up through them and telling us of things to be. "For," he says, "we know not what we should pray for as we ought, but the Spirit itself prays in us." It is He that prays, not we, in sighs which are inarticulate — that is, in aspirations which are not our private petitions, but the prophecyings of God out of the deeps of our suffering humanity.

A truth here dawns upon us, whose sweep and significance are of the greatest moment. It is none other than the immanence of God in human nature; his prophecyings in us and the pledges of the Divine veracity for their fulfillment.

Following out this doctrine of the Apostle, we distinguish in the human heart two classes of desires: one class human, one class Divine, or inspirations of the Divine. There are those which are simply personal, which relate to my own private affairs, bodily appetites, worldly comforts, animal wants, personal expectations and plans. They are the reachings out of the selfhood after its own gratifications. These God has not pledged Himself always to fulfill. On the other hand He crosses them, denies them, mortifies them, sometimes entirely subdues and overcomes them. These are not his voice in us. They are our own private and personal cries, sometimes answered, sometimes not, according as it comports with our own and the common weal. And there are some, undoubtedly, who have no other desires than these, and who never pray heartily for aught but personal favors. What helps them on in this world and makes them personally prosperous is all they wish or ask for. All the world is going right provided their selfhood be ministered unto and fed and pampered. All the world is going wrong if this be not so. And so the Divine breathing, as it comes in deep sighs through human nature, like wind murmuring through groves of pine, has never been felt in their consciousness.

But to all persons who have the first-fruits of the Spirit, on whose natures the Christian Gospel has had even the beginnings of its operation, there are sighings and aspirations quite other than these. They transcend the little sphere of self and personal interest. They originate not in us. They strike into us and roll out again, faint and feeble, or full and strong, as you are fitted to receive and give them out, — like an organ of sweet stops when struck or played upon from another hand. These are what Paul means by the intercessions of the Spirit in breathings which are inarticulate. Let us distinguish them ; and as we distinguish this voice of God in us from our personal cries and selfish clamors, a twofold lesson will come to us as we proceed. What then are the breathings upward which come from the immanence of God in human souls ?

I. First, there are the hopes of immortality. True, the hope of a future life may be a selfish hope. Not so, however, when we crave it as a prolonged and enlarged sphere of angelic activities already begun. Addison's argument for the future life is from the expectations which God implanted, and which, therefore, He cannot disappoint. But it is more than this you perceive in the grand apostolic argument, more than mere continuous existence. See how he puts it. The whole creation sighs and travails in pain, waiting for the redemption of our body. You perceive it is not continuous existence merely which the Apostle has in view. It is existance freed from these clogs and hindrances and limitations. It is the redemption of our body, so that from being a drag, it shall become the fit organism of the soul. Have you not wondered sometimes at the arrangements and economies of this life ; why so much of our time is taken up in getting bread, and raiment, and shelter for the body ; why that is made our most absorbing care, and to so many people almost their sole concern; why even the glories of sky and landscape are made secondary to their ministrations to bodily wants; why Nature's secret laboratories are broken into and searched, not so much to get openings upward as to get some medicine for man's poor infirmities and bruises? Very strange it would be, except that this earth was designed only as the very rudiments of being, the mere chrysalis of our existence. Very strange it would be, except that this veil of flesh and matter was designed to conceal from us more than it discloses, and only give us hints, suggestions, and tantalizing gleams. It is the Divine plan first to excite longings and hungerings before God fills us with good. Indeed, the hungerings must come first, else the good cannot be relished, or even received. Therefore it is that here He has barred us in and balked us in a thousand ways, cumbered with gross bodies, and very mean ones at that, yet given us vanishing glimpses of a better state, that He may awaken these sighings and expectations. Such are the aspirations of immortality. They come not till a state of being has dawned upon our faith transcending so much the highest perfection of this, that its faintest twilight shall show us more of the Divine Beauty than earth's most refulgent noon.

I remember that when a child, I used to play almost within the giant shadows of the Taghconic Mountains, and sometimes stop and look up at that great wall of blue that stood sharp against the sky, and wonder what lay over beyond it. The wonder and longing increased with years, the more so as I watched the setting sunlight round up the highest peak and disappear, indicating, as it would seem, an ocean of gold surging up from the other side ; till I broke away one day and climbed up there, through bush and brier, and stood on the summit and looked over into the unimaginable and glorious Beyond. That discipline is just what God is doing for us here in these valleys of time with the light of eternity playing on the highest peaks that hem us in. The Christian faith has not dawned upon you with any clearness unless it has so exalted and brightened all your ideals of the Divine glory that this earth grows very dim and shadowy even in its summer robes and holidays ; and then come the breathings inarticulate which Paul describes ; aspirations towards a perfection and a beauty which transcend those of the senses ; the foretellings of the soul as struck by the Spirit of God on whose line of aspirations she rises to their fulfillment as faith turns to sight and hope is lost in Reality.

Is there any heart here that sighs for a better state? Is there any mind on which has dawned the blessed ideals of a perfection unrealized ; of a fellowship more full and sufficing than you get here ; of more heartfelt communion with Christ ; of the exercise of a more swift angelic beneficence? These are not your sighings, but breathings of God through you, and telling you of things to be. They are not private prophecyings, but the touch of God's finger on the human lyre, waking sighs for redemption, and giving openings of paradise. They awaken sighs and longings, because in the nature of things God must give us hunger before He gives us food : the thirst must come before the slaking, and yearnings after higher perfection must come to you before you enter the land where there is no trail of the serpent over its green.

II. Somewhat different from this, yet intimately connected with it, are breathings after holiness. These again are not your private desires, but the Spirit praying in you and through you. How selfish sometimes are our prayers !— prayers even for salvation, when by being saved is only meant some outward good vicariously bestowed and purchased. But breathings after holiness, or heaven as a subjective state of purity and divine order within you are quite otherwise. And He has girded us with sin and pollution, and made us vividly conscious of them, and then put his own Spirit within us for the end of showing our corruption in contrast with his own purity, that we may sigh for the holiness of God. And you observe that according to the apostolic doctrine these breathings for holiness are the pledge of fulfillment. They are the Spirit prophecying — not we — therefore God's promise that He will make us clean if only we desire it. If you desire cleanness of heart, it is the sure pledge that you will have it; for it is God promising. Those who are always satisfied, who are complacent in their worldliness, the angels themselves might despair of. As to purity of heart and life, the same law must hold ever and everywhere; the thirst must come before the slaking, the hunger before the food: the awful chasm between our corruption and God's purity must be seen before He will come over to us and bring forth his best robe and put it on us.

III. Once more we analyze, and we find in every soul which has been born of the Spirit a sentiment which stands apart from all our selfish wants and clamorings. It is the desire to serve others; to do something for the common weal, something, however humble, that shall increase the sum total of human happiness, and that shall tend to redeem the world from evil and restore it to a full communion with its Lord. It is this sentiment which inspires every missionary enterprise and sends the Howards and the Judsons over the earth as the angels of heavenly mercy. It is this which prompts all our praying for each other, and all our deeds of disinterested love. The motions of the Spirit within, and its forthgoings in prayers and activities for human redemption, are its intercessions for the salvation of all mankind. In one of his sublime moods the Apostle hears the low breathing of the whole creation going up in moanings and pleadings for deliverance, as if the universal Spirit had made all nature and all humanity an instrument to play upon, and whose minor keys sent up to the ear of God tones of pity and wailing for human woe. It is the universe travailing in pain at the touch of the Divine hand upon its heart-strings; it is God's Spirit breathing through it and coming up again to his ear in one universal prayer for restoration to its Lord. The older churches have prayers for the dead, assuming, and very justly too, that death does not sunder the ties of a common brotherhood; and unless you allow the assumption of our extreme Protestantism, that as soon as we die our state is fixed eternally and cannot change, no reason appears why we should not pray for them still. The happiness of heaven itself must have an element of disturbance, — must lack completeness, to say the least, so long as the wail of suffering rises from below to mingle with its songs, with no effort or desire to mitigate and save.

IV. But the sermon would not be faithful without another application. There is in all men a sense or a faculty which they call conscience. By common consent it is regarded as standing apart in the consciousness — the Shekinah which the Lord keeps in our nature, whence his light flashes out to warn and to guide us. We will not pause to analyze it now; but if you have attended to the state of your own mind when the conscience was responding in tones of reproach to violations of the Divine Law, you have found something more than a sense of right and wrong. You have found mingled with your regret and self-reproach an apprehension of something to come.

The conscience is always prophetic. It looks before as well as after. Hence, so many who have denied bibles and revelations from without for the sake of getting a sense of security in sin, have been startled by fore-gleams from within, shining down into chasms of a coming retribution. We may deny the written Bible; we may mistake its meaning; we may be bewildered by false religions. But the fact remains, that God has so formed our very nature and so pitched and tuned it, that when you lay profane hands on the instrument you are answered by a voice that rolls in startling distinctness, down even the long and shadowy aisles of an eternal world, and the scenery of a coming judgment. It is not man speaking, but God speaking out of man, — the Spirit immanent in you, not merely telling you what is right and what is wrong, but holding you to a coming retribution and refusing to let you go. It is God speaking through you, foretelling a judgment to come, since He is not a man that He should lie, nor the son of man that He should repent.

I have read of a man who reasoned himself into atheism and crime, but coming to the verge of this mortal life was awakened by the loud prophecies of the Spirit within. It was not fear of a local hell somewhere in the uncertain future, but hell already realized, and flinging its lurid gleams through the shadows of the coming darkness. "That which triumphs," said he, "within the jaws of immortality is doubtless immortal; and as for a Deity, nothing less than an Almighty could inflict what I feel." Terrible arguments these! The voice of God striking through us, but rolling out of us again, down through the abysses of eternity. Better be persuaded of a God by willing obedience to his Christ, than by the prophecies of a violated conscience, sounding on through the portals that open downward into the night.

One lesson let me draw from the subject, and that we will lay up and carry home with us. Some people are always doubting and hesitating about prayer. Why should we pray at all since God knows our wants before we ask Him? You see in the light of this subject that those who have the Spirit of the Lord in them pray because they cannot help it; for when you get beyond the circle of mere selfish desires his Spirit prays in you and urges you mightily. Longings for higher attainment as the bright ideals go on before you and beckon you upward; breathing after holiness when in the light of God's dazzling purity you are sick of your own sin, — when these come to you, you will pray every day and every hour, and what is more, be sure of an answer.

I think one of the most blessed boons which the Gospel bestows on the human race is the clear annunciation of a principle that takes all servility out of worship, and all selfishness out of prayer; this principle, namely, that the desire of salvation, if you have it, renders it impossible you should ever miss of salvation — as impossible as it is for God to break his word. Only do not make a mistake as to what salvation means. It means a clean heart and a heavenly mind. It is not heaven as the scenery of rivers and landscapes, though doubtless all that may be, but heaven as a subjective state of Christ-like disposition and affections.

Whoever desires these and prays for them, the prayer renders it impossible he shall miss the attainment, since it is the Holy Spirit praying and prophesying within. It is thus that every one who asketh, receiveth, and he who seeketh, findeth. The annunciation of this one law of asking and receiving, of prayer and its answer, puts the Gospel in heavenly contrast with human substitutes for the Gospel; and, if once you have a firm grasp upon it, is sufficient to take all gloom from religion, to put into it the elasticity of faith and hope, yea, to hang all the clouds of life with rainbows.

THE THREE ADVENTS.

THE Eternal Word came down from heaven
  Wrapped in our human clay;
Beneath his voice the tombs were riven
  And searched with blaze of day.

He comes again — the Spirit's power,
  On soft and dove-like wing;
I breathe in this thy advent hour
  The balmiest gales of Spring!

And when thy voice, like thunders loud,
  Brings on the judgment day,
And through this intervening cloud
  Doth cleave thy shining way,

Let thy white robe of righteousness
  Our trusting souls adorn,
And be the shinings of thy face
  The eternal Christmas Morn!

VII.

THE GOSPEL CONTRASTS.

MATTHEW xxv. 46. *These shall go away into everlasting punishment: but the righteous into life eternal.*

THE arrangement of the words in the original text is so made that the two members of the sentence are put in balance one against the other. Thus, "These shall go away into *punishment* eternal, but the righteous into *life* eternal." This word rendered "punishment" means, according to its etymology, a particular kind of punishment. Literally it means pruning — as the pruning of trees. It suggests the idea that the punishment is not arbitrary or revengeful, but disciplinary and corrective; for you do not prune trees for the purpose of destroying them, but to remove hindrances and morbid growths. The passage has often been regarded as if the chief thing to be considered was the *duration* of the punishment of the unrighteous, over against the duration of the life of the righteous; and that since both are described by the same word they are of like duration. That would undoubtedly be so if mere duration or extension by time were expressed at all, or any way involved in the contrast. But that, as I should interpret, is not the meaning of the original word. The element of time as we measure things does not enter into it at all. Not duration, but quality, is the chief thing involved in this word rendered "eternal." If I should say one man's state is heavenly and another man's is fiendish, I should put their qualities in contrast, without reference to their duration. So here in the contrast between the punishment of the unrighteous and the life of the righteous. The word which qualifies them does not mean measurement by our standards of time, whether endless or not. It means rather a punishment and a life beyond time and all its changes and estimates. The eternal life is promised the saints now and here, but they may forfeit it and fall away from it nevertheless. So I should paraphrase the words thus: These shall go away into a punishment which time cannot measure, and the righteous into a life which time cannot measure; that is, which is out of time and beyond its bourne.

This whole discourse, running through two chapters, the twenty-fourth and twenty-fifth, has always seemed to me the most remarkable that ever fell from human lips. It is one of those utterances which avouch their own origin, and which break through all the discoursings of men as a peal of thunder from the heavens hushes the noises of the street and compels us to listen. That Matthew, or anybody else, put it in of himself, that the literary exploit of any age is up to a level of that kind, were about as reasonable to my mind as to suppose that some telegraph operator had become so expert as to invent the lightnings, or so mimic their course on the sky that none could distinguish the real ones from the flashy imitations. Not that this discourse of our Saviour deals mainly in the terrific, or in appeals to human fears. It has passages so full of tenderness that it would seem as if the very heart of the Divine Mercy were breaking for the woes of men; and in these last passages that announce the Divine judgments, there is a humanity that swells and throbs through the sentences: as when He speaks of the hungry, the naked, the prisoners, all of God's humble poor, and says mercy to them is the same as mercy to me, for I suffer with them.

The word αἰών and its derivatives, rendered "eternal" and "everlasting," describe an economy complete in itself, and the duration must depend on the nature of the economy. What then do the Scriptures reveal to us? The results of this temporal economy in the one that lies next on, beyond the limits of the first death. They lift the curtain, and in the solemn porches of eternity they show us the human current parting divers ways to the realms of light and the realms of darkness. The New Testament, if it reveals anything, reveals the αἰών — the dispensation that lies next to this, and gathers into it the momentous results of our probation in time. But what lies beyond *that* in the cycles of a coming eternity, I do not believe has been revealed to the highest angel. Think of that endless Beyond! If every atom of the globe were counted off and every atom stood for a million years, still we have not approached a conception of endless duration. And yet sinful and fallible men affirm that their fellow sinners are to be given over to indescribable agonies through those millions of years thus repeated, and even then the clocks of eternity have only struck the morning hour! that the hells of pent-up anguish are to streak eternity with blood in lines parallel forever with the being of God! If Gabriel should come and tell us that, we should have a right to believe that the history of the infinite future infolded in the bosom of God had not been given to Gabriel!

A candid and reasonable interpretation, while it has not told and cannot tell what lies beyond the cycle which Scripture reveals, may and does give us clearer views of the *nature* of retribution. All the scenery of the spirit-world described in the Bible is to be understood in the light of a more rational pneumatology. Because it is not material scenery, it none the less sets forth the most august realities, the things contained already in human nature and waiting to be disclosed. The future of man he bears within himself — the white enrobing purities, and the fires and the ascending smoke of torment. It is a most instructive fact that conceptions of the future retribution always tally exactly with one's intuitions of moral evil. Any man who thinks sin belongs only to the surface, will see very little or no evil in prospect when this outward coil has been removed. Any man in whose consciousness moral and spiritual evil have been more vivid, and its subtle and malignant nature understood, will readily believe that the lowest hells which the Scriptures describe are no rhetorical exaggerations, but the real apocalypse of an uncleansed human nature. He knows that since this tide of humanity is setting into the spiritual world continually, with only portions of it redeemed from evil, there must be in that world the heights of peace and the noxious abysses which no plummet can fathom, and he will not try to hide the reality in shallow sentimentalism. For what is here concealed under temporal disguises, must there be open and palpable where the disguises are swept away. Three stages of enlightenment on this subject may be thus described. In the ante-Christian period there were faint gleams and guess-work. In the first Christian period the fact is disclosed, the imagery of heaven and hell is unveiled with marvelous distinctness, but understood as localities of space and time. But in the stage of more rational interpretation they are the symbolization of the things in man to break forth in open manifestation.

With these preliminary considerations, let us endeavor to get the essential meaning of these gospel contrasts, summed up in the text as the contrast between eternal (αἰώνιον) life and eternal punishment, more often described as the contrast between life and death. In so doing, I am persuaded we shall come to the heart and substance of the Gospel message.

All life in man is measured by the intensity and vividness of the consciousness. Life in its fullness means strength and quickness in all the faculties. Take for illustration the lowest plane, which is the sensuous life. In some people the senses are clear and quick, and they will put one in swift communication with all the beauty and all the facts that lie about him. We say then he is alive to what is around him. The ear drinks in the smallest wavelets of sound. The eye sees; and color, size, proportion, outline, distance, things far and near, and great and small, are keenly discerned. The touch takes swift cognition in the thrilling nerves. And so of all the senses. One man will pass through a few miles of space and be so alive to what is in it that volumes will not exhaust his narrative. And you can imagine these senses so alive as to see worlds of wonder and glory right about us which have never disclosed themselves to us as yet because we are too dull to take them in, — under our feet, over head, in all the air, — mysteries that lie at the heart of things waiting to be disclosed. One of the fathers of astronomy, opposed by the bigots of his day, exults at the marvels which opened to his keener vision, and he exclaims with rapture : " I can wait two hundred years for a reader since God waited six thousand years for an observer ! "

Again, the senses may be dull and half-dead, so that a man may perceive very little of what is about him. He will go through the same miles of space and see nothing and hear nothing that some animals would not see and hear. A man begins to die bodily when his senses begin to fail, and when they fail altogether he *is* dead, and all this scene of sights and sounds exists for him no more.

It is precisely so with the spiritual life and with all the faculties of the soul. The reason may be clear as a mirror to receive the truth, and its step strong and unerring to reach its conclusions. Faith may grasp its objects so royally that things future may be as things that are. The affections may be so full, and so warm and flowing, that the soul shall be drawn to the good and the true as the lover to his bride. The conscience may be so clear and responsive that the voice of God shall fill the soul as with the sound of " flutes and soft recorders." And the power of execution may be so nimble that a man's works shall be like radiating charities. Such a soul is alive ; and you see how one man may live in a world from which another man right by his side is barred and excluded altogether.

And now we can see what eternal life means. It is life on a higher plane of being and in the higher degrees of the mind ; the best faculties made so vivid and active that eternal things are open to them, and their glories revealed. What is the life of heaven? Not that of lazy devotion, but the human powers raised to such a pitch of intensity that the Spirit and the love of God fill them to the full ; the reason, an outlook into divine and angelic being ; affections so burning that love never waxes cold ; charity an overflowing stream that never dries up ; faith so assured that prayer always lays the soul on the bosom of its Lord. This is life. Because it puts the soul into the enjoyment and communion with eternal things, and opens to it the highest landscapes of eternity, it is called the eternal life, and because unlike our temporal life it is unfluctuating and perennial. The element of time does not enter into it at all. You cannot measure it by months and years though they were endless. Suppose the life of an animal, or of a sensuous man, to be prolonged forever ; that is not the eternal life of the Gospel. Suppose the agonies of mortality to be prolonged forever ; that is not the eternal death of the Gospel, nor any approach towards its conception. It is life and death on the higher planes of being, out of time and out of space, and which they cannot measure, though extended without end. It is this that the Scriptures describe by the untranslatable word αἰώνιον.

We observe, again, that enjoyment corresponds with the measure of life which one possesses. A clod or a stone enjoys nothing because they are not alive. Some animals are but just removed from vegetable existence, and their life is so torpid that they may be killed without much pain. Men who have not much life enjoy little and suffer little. They slug rather than live. But when the consciousness becomes intense, the sensibilities keen, and the affections warm, what a flood of enjoyment, of glory, and of beauty rushes in upon them, even from this lower universe! The freedom of the city of God is theirs. All pleasure, all happiness, come from the activity of the faculties, putting them in full correspondence with their objects.

Such, then, is the eternal life. These conceptions, it is true, do not agree with the notion which makes heaven a place of indolent repose, or listless devotion, into which we can be introduced by vicarious or legal arrangements. But in the very nature of things, the state of the highest bliss is where the soul in all her faculties is raised to such a pitch of activity and quickness of perception that she inherits all things. She is not introduced among them passively. They open upon her as her own powers become enlarged and unlocked to take them in and enjoy them.

II. We now come to the opposite term, death, or as we have it in the text, punishment, or pruning away. Death, as the opposite of life, is the waning and falling away of the human powers. It is not the extinguishment of existence. I think it is never used in Scripture as synonymous with annihilation. It is the going down of existence towards the clods of the valley. A man, I said, begins to die physically when his senses begin to grow dull and shut him in from the natural world. The eye fails, the ear fails, the touch fails, all the avenues from without fail, and things around grow blurred and dim. Finally they close altogether, and then the comely form lies there a corpse — the cold effigy of a man, and all sights and sounds pass over it as they do over the stones and the trees. There is a bright universe above it and around it, but the decayed senses have shut it all out.

Just so it is with spiritual death. All sin tends to weaken the faculties and blunt their perceptions, and finally to close them up. It is so with sensual sin. Violate the beautiful laws of this bodily frame, and how much more quickly will its senses become feeble and dull, ending sometimes in the paralysis of its nerves. So of reason and the moral sense, and the kindly sympathies and the power of seeing and acquiring divine truth. Sin makes them wane and die out. And then the whole spiritual man is dead, and the heavenly world is shut out from his perceptions and his enjoyments, simply because he has no faculty to put him in correspondence with them, or even to assure him that they exist. He is dead to them as a corpse is dead to nature. Hence you find all through the Bible that the consequences of sin are represented not as suffering imposed *upon* the sinner, but as an inhering destruction and decline. It is death, destruction, perishing, darkness, pruning away; and the meaning is, not annihilation, but that it tends to make all positive existence fade out till the sinful become the negatives of real men. "Except ye repent ye shall all likewise perish," — for to perish is to wither away into a husk or a shell. This is spiritual death. Hell then is a negative state, not positive. It is the night side of the universe. It is humanity reversed and turned away from the central glory. Whereas heaven is positive, — man turned towards God, humanity on the day-side receiving the warmth and radiance of the Divine Nature and bringing forth fruit under its inspiring energy.

III. We come to another truth. The more of life there is to die out, the greater is the convulsion and the agony. It is so with the body, and it is so with the soul. If the human frame is full of strength and energy, its death struggle is more intense. So of the death of the soul. Man has an angel's faculties. They cannot be wrenched away from their high end and go down in darkness without long and fearful agonies. You see it so here when the soul is preyed upon by the unclean passions which the Scriptures call the infernal fire. The relief from this is only in the decay of the capacity for suffering which sin, unrepented of, produces at last, — the fire of the soul burning out its purer and nobler material, and leaving a blackened crater to be filled with snow. Endless *torture* is an impossibility and a contradiction in terms; for torture destroys finally even the capacity for feeling torture, and eats out the material it feeds on. Neither annihilation nor endless suffering are implied in the second death, but the waste and desolation of a soul which has lost the capacity to enjoy or to suffer greatly, — though none may tell the mental agony through which an immortal mind must pass to that awful ruin. Physical suffering is of no account compared with those inward tortures which are independent of the bodily senses. Hence when all external arrangements are propitious and fair, the soul within may be wrung from a deeper seat of anguish than mortal weapons can ever reach; and the anguish has sometimes been so great that men have rushed on death, in the hope of escaping from it. In his higher nature man neither enjoys nor suffers like an animal. There is a tone in his rapture which is not of earth, and a tone that is more than mortal mingles in the voice of his wail.

Reasoning thus from the analogies which give us most surely and directly the significance of language, we evolve the meaning of these contrasts of the Christian revelation. They indicate a retribution of the most solemn import to be wrought out on the higher planes of being. They point to a state of existence beyond this present, where every man shall reap down the harvest which he sows. Of what lies on beyond *that* I will not speculate now I do not know of any *written* revelation pertaining to that endless Beyond of sinful men. There are unwritten intimations in the hopes and aspirations which the Spirit inspires and which go up in prayers and intercessions for the redemption and final happiness of every immortal soul. These, as we saw in the last discourse, are not merely our private praying, but the prophecyings of the Spirit through us and telling us of things to be; for I will not believe that our private praying is more humane than the Eternal Spirit that inspires it. It warrants the belief that there will be no unnecessary pang in the universe, or down the eternities, though it does not reveal to us the epoch or the methods of the final restoration. Such a revelation, thrown down upon us externally, might interfere, perhaps, with the best achievements of our probation now and here. There is enough revealed to disclose the fearful nature and consequences of sin; for the rest, I trust to the Infinite goodness without seeking for that which is held in the Divine Reserve.

(1.) Two points in the conclusion are urged upon

us. The mission of Christ and the nature of his salvation reveal themselves to us with great clearness. "I have come," He says, "that ye might have life, and that ye might have it more abundantly." He gives life because He imparts inward energy. He comes not to repress and cripple the reason, but to enlarge it, strengthen it, open wide its eye-sight, and lift it up into divine illuminations. He comes to unlock the deepest fountains of love and make them flow, and this He does by turning upon us all the Divine graces and charms. He comes to make the moral sense so lively and responsive that its vibrations shall fill the soul with angelic harmonies. He comes to fortify the will and make it like flint for the right and the true. He comes to strengthen the power of doing and give us drafts on God's omnipotence for godlike achievement. He comes not to purchase heaven for us — so much blood for so much salvation — but so to build up the man within through living faith, and so to open out his mind to all the good in the universe, that it shall be heaven to him wherever he moves ; not to crush the faculties under fear and cowardice, but to touch every one with a divine impulse, and make it go with gladness to its work. "He that believeth on me *hath* everlasting life, and I will raise him up at the last day."

(2.) Again, the nature of Christ's Church, and why it is a Church militant and aggressive, and not dormant and passive, becomes obvious in the light of our subject. It is because in the former there is life, and scope for the putting forth and enlargement of all the powers of an immortal being ; whereas in passivity and asceticism the faculties fall away and go down towards death. If you hear truly and distinctly " the voice of the Son of Man," it will be to you a trumpet call to active duty and not a lull into solitary rest. It is the trump that wakes the sleepers from their graves to a resurrection of life, lest if they sleep on it will be to a resurrection of damnation. The highest peace, that which alone is eternal, is won through power. More than ever the voice of the great Head of the Church is sounding through it. " The time is coming, and now is, when the dead shall hear the voice of the Son of Man, and they that hear shall be alive."

A SONG IN THE MINOR KEY.

I STAND on Time's mysterious brink,
  And send an onward gaze
Where throngs of spirits rise or sink
  At parting of the ways.

Upward, towards the sun-lit rooms,
  They climb the shining stairs;
Or, downward through the swirling glooms,
  Sink to their long despairs.

And happy thrills of song and lyre
  Come from the angel-train,
And upward through the crater-fire
  The muffled groans of pain.

And as I heard, my song uprose
  To catch that heavenly air,
When straightway on my lips it froze
  To agonizing prayer.

O ye who climb the stairs above,
  And crowd up nigh the throne,
How can ye sing redeeming Love
  And see its work half done?

O thou great Mercy! folding all
  Beneath thy brooding wing, —
Those who to thee for pity call
  Or their redemption sing, —

I ask not through the highest room
  Of heavenly state to go,
But downward through the thickest gloom
  Of any child of woe.

Did not thy Christ go down to hell
  And cut its brazen bars,
Before he sought his coronal —
  His golden crown of stars?

Are they not all my kith and kin,
  And children, Lord, of thine,
Alike who beg in rags of sin, —
  In jeweled robes who shine?

We all are beggars; poor and bare
  We stand before thy face,
Save when in borrowed robes we flare,
  Or shinings of thy grace.

Here I will raise no song of glee,
  And hold no waving palm;
I breathe upon the minor key
  My penitential psalm.

I share my brother's grief — I list
  The undertones of pain,
And pray to see thy conquering Christ
  Go up with all his train.

VIII.

TREADING THE WINE-PRESS.

ISAIAH lxiii. 3. *I have trodden the wine-press alone.*

THIS sentence is from one of those chapters of the old prophecies which are generally understood to foreshadow the Messiah. But as foreshadowed here, he is not the temporal prince nor the conquering hero of the Jewish imagination. It seems to me, in reading these chapters, that the future Christ had arisen on the vision of the prophet in his true character and his moral grandeur, and that the prophet is straining his vision to get it clear of Jewish hallucinations. A form rises away in the distant perspective, which he cannot present to his reader in any such outline as the painter gives to his picture, or the sculptor to his statue, partly because it is beyond finite conception, and partly because the vista is filled with Jewish haze. A character is sketched, nevertheless, such as had never appeared in history, and with such combination of attributes and qualities as no writer would sketch from his own fancy. He is divine, yet human; triumphant, yet weak and suffering; royal, yet with no lineage that men can trace; glorious in his apparel, yet with no comeliness that men can desire; treading down his enemies, yet drawing upon Himself the sorrows and iniquities of all. But there is nothing more striking in the whole portraiture than the lonely greatness of the man. He stands out solitary. He treads the wine-press alone. His height is so great that it lifts him away from kindred sympathies and ties. A chasm lies between Him and all other men, and between Him and God, for He is stricken and afflicted of God himself.

The Christ is the only being who ever filled up this vast foreshadowing with historic reality. And no fact in the Saviour's life is more strangely impressive than this of his absolute solitude. For what solitude is like that of being alone in the midst of crowds, among a great company, and yet so wide apart from it that the distance between is altogether impassable. He drew around Him a band of disciples and believers; but the one that stood nearest, and leaned on his breast, remained in almost total ignorance of the being he followed, until after his death and resurrection. He stood under a heavy load of mortal anguish, when there was no one to help Him bear it, or even to know it was laid upon Him. The gulf of separation even came between Him and the Eternal Father. And when the load was heaviest, and He went away by Himself and fell beneath it, no mortal was a witness to it, and even his disciples were fast asleep.

No solitude is like his. And yet it represents a

condition of human nature. For this very reason the Saviour bore the trial, that He might come to every one else who has the same trial to bear, and clothe him with strength from on high. For every one of us must bear it in our place and degree. The longer we live, and the more our being becomes individualized, the more shall we find ourselves alone. Every man is separated from every other man, and probably no person was ever perfectly understood by any other person. There are common tastes and feelings and sympathies; but at the same time there is an individualism that keeps apart, and refuses to yield itself to the crowd. No one knows his fellow a great way beneath the surface. There is something in you that has never been disclosed to your neighbor who sits beside you,— something in him to which you are a stranger, and with which you cannot intermeddle. Looks, language, actions reveal a little, but there is that in every one which finds not a symbol nor a tongue.

This fact has a very important bearing on the whole subject of human trial. As your eye rests on almost any group of people whom accident may have brought together, you would see ordinarily nothing but cheerful appearances and salutations. If the concourse were gathered from what are usually called the favored classes,— those, namely, who are not subjected to the hard necessities of toil, and have abundant leisure for enjoyment,— you will find, perhaps, not only cheerfulness, but hilarity and gayety. Happy people! you would say. They taste the sweet without the bitter; they drink the wine of life without the lees.

But could you follow that concourse as they separate one by one, and part off each to his own place and home; could you enter that home, and look back through the continuous line of its history, you would generally find that each went to some place of sorrowful recollections; that in the sunshine of every house there was a blank spot, or it may be the outlines of a fearful shadow. I do not say that this will always be found true, at any one moment, of all the families you might name, but I say it is true of every family before its history is wound up. Not a hearthstone shall you find on which some shadow has not fallen or is about to fall. Further than this, you will probably find that there are few households which do not cherish some sorrow not known to the world; who have not some trial which is their peculiar messenger, and which they do not talk about except among themselves. Some hope that has been blasted; some expectation dashed down; some wrong, real or supposed, which some member of the household has suffered; trembling anxieties lest that other member will not succeed; trials from the peculiar temperament of somebody in the house, or some environment that touches it sharply from without; some thorn in the flesh;

some physical disability that cripples our energies when we want to use them the most; some spot in the house where Death has left his track, or painful listenings to hear his stealthy footsteps coming on: these, and a thousand other things, render it certain that there is no house which must not some day have a secret shadow on its hearth.

Further than this, even; there is no individual whose experience has any breadth and depth, who has not some trial which you know nothing about, and which perhaps no one knows but himself. This we may assume, — partly from the fact that there are struggles of the hidden life where none but God can be a helper; that there are doubts, fears, tremblings, disappointments, combats, hopes that rise and fall; which always gather about it, — partly, too, from the fact that the most pungent and wasting sorrows to which the human heart becomes a prey are the very ones which retire farthest inward and refuse even to be breathed into the ear of friendship. For the hardest trials of all are those of the spiritual nature, where every man wrestles with his own temptations, which are different from any other man's, and give him an experience which is all his own, and which no one can understand but himself; where even the best men, to all outward seeming, have felt that desertion which the Christ had when he prayed the Father not to forsake him, and where sometimes the great conflict of life goes on beneath the glare which grandeur or station has thrown around it.

I assume it, then, as an undeniable fact, that while there are vast inequalities in appearances touching our natural allotments of joy and sorrow, yet when you lay off these appearances and come to the naked facts of the case, it is quite otherwise. The secret trials of human hearts put them on ground of equality before God. And though no man's trials are just like any other man's yet they are all his own, and every soul has its own secret burden to bear. There are common griefs and condolences ; yet after all these have been talked over, each has something left which he has not shared with his neighbor, and that may be the very thing that touches him most nearly and tenderly. So that, while there are common burdens to be borne and common consolations to be shared, it is also true in a most important sense, that every man must tread the wine-press alone.

Let us now see if we cannot derive some very important lessons from this economy of things. What are the teachings of these secret trials ?

I. The first is this, — to cease from all those false comparisons that breed discontents and envyings amongst men. Almost every individual, at some period of his life, seems to himself to be separated by Divine Providence to some peculiar hardship, and he wonders why this is so. Why am I singled out, and thrust beyond the circle of Divine favors ? Why is it that I have this burden laid upon me, while this other individual and that other family send forth their little ones like a flock, and their children dance? Very likely, if his feelings were candidly analyzed, he would find himself at issue both with his neighbor and his God, because while he had failed, some one else had succeeded, and outstripped him in the race of life. He does not remember that appearances serve as a protection to keep out the glare of the world from the sacred privacies of the heart. If the protecting coverings were all swept away under which each one struggles with his lot and treads the wine-press alone, every pretext for envy or discontent on this score would disappear, and every man would see that every other man was separated to some burden quite as peculiar as his own.

And here we have room to remark on the admirable compensations of the Divine Providence. Every man has his own adversary to struggle with apart, and his own victory to gain, for the simple reason that God designs to educe from our diversified experience every variety of the graces and virtues. He never repeats Himself in nature; but from the cedar of Lebanon to the lily of the vale, He seeks a fresh evolution and efflorescence out of his own grandeur and beauty, that infinite diversity may make up the infinite completeness and harmony. Just so it is in human character and moral attainment. God never repeats Himself here. He gives to each a varied experience. We march not in serried numbers to conquer a common foe, but He leads us through separate paths, each one to struggle with his own adversary alone, that, when the victory is gained, and the crown is won, each shall have in it a leaf or a chaplet which is unlike any other, so that all together may reflect every possible hue of the Divine loveliness.

II. A second lesson comes to us from these secret trials. If the fact were pondered and appreciated as it should be, it would strengthen very much that bond of sympathy and brotherhood which ought to exist among all the members of the social state. I doubt whether in this our earthly condition, we ever come to the full *feeling* of sympathy and brotherhood, without the consciousness of a common frailty and sorrow. You may reason with men very finely, plying the argument that we have one Father, that we are all partakers of his nature, and therefore are all brethren. Very true, but men will not care for it in the day of their strength and pride, and you never will melt any man's heart towards his fellows by mere beautiful theorizing. But suppose some common calamity were to sweep over these people and bend them low; suppose some angel of sorrow were to pass over every house and leave his victim; it would do more, a thousand times, to make every man feel that he is a part of every other man than all our fine philosophy. But what I have put as hypothesis is simple and sober fact, though the fact is veiled under thin and artificial disguises, for I say to you that the angel does pass over every house and leave his victim; and if you could draw the curtain aside, you would see he had been treading the wine-press behind it.

It was found when one of the great ocean steamers was on the verge of shipwreck, the passengers, who represented almost every sect in Christendom, and who before had kept apart in groups, forgot all their sectarianism in the presence of a common danger, and they knelt and prayed together as one family in Christ, about to be summoned to his bar. Precisely so it would be in the great voyage of life. Let the fact be fully pondered, that there is no Utopian independence of the common lot, that there is a woe that presses down separately on every man's soul, and that he, like myself, is wrestling hard with it, though it comes to each man in variant shape, and suited to his condition, — let this be pondered as it should be, and every man will look upon every other man as bound to himself by a more interesting and tender tie. Yea, when I meet the man of show and equipage, I shall not be found gazing so much on the glitter and the gilding, as musing with myself how it fares with that man under the protecting shadows where he treads the wine-press alone.

There was a fierce battle fought, and a victory won; and foremost in the battle, and most honored in the rejoicings of victory, was a brave old count whose heart and arm seemed both to be made of steel. The feast is over and the rejoicings are hushed, and the stillness of night has come down upon the plain. But lo! there is a taper burning in the tent of the iron count, while all but the guard have gone to rest. Why sleeps he not upon his laurels? Why burns his lamp at midnight after the day has covered him with glory? They lift a corner of the curtain and look in, and the iron count sits alone over the body of his dead son, and great drops are standing in his eyes. A German poet has described it, and a German painter has put it upon canvas. And it describes very well what takes place after most of the conflicts of life, after the victory is won and the festivities are over, and the chief man among them treads the wine-press alone.

III. A third lesson, and still more important. For aught that yet appears, there need have been no burden to any man which others might not share, no grief of the heart which he might not tell to his neighbor. And yet every man is separated to his own burden. Each has a reserved fund of trouble, which to him is a special dispensation. Now see the necessity of this! If I could share everything with my fellow, I should have nothing left to share specially and sacredly with Him who bends his ear from the heavens for this very purpose. I should come to depend altogether on human aid; in which case my mind would go out laterally to my fellows, and not upward continually unto God. Every trial which you have that other people cannot understand ought to be a secret tie that binds you more closely and indissolubly to the throne. I doubt whether God ever won a soul to heaven on which He had not first let fall some separate drops of grief, which from their very nature are a secret between the soul and her God. This holds especially true of that sense of unworthiness, that haunting conviction of sinfulness, or a spiritual nature unrestored, which to many minds is the most pungent of all hidden sorrows, and which from its very profundity no one can share and few can comprehend. It is in these grapplings with some secret woe, where all human help is unavailing and where no human eye must look in, that the soul lays hold mightily upon God, and the strengthening angel comes down to her, and she finally prevails, and puts on victory like a robe. This is the highest meaning, and this the grand result of all secret trials rightly improved. I doubt whether any saint who has now passed on and holds the waving palm in his hand, without this economy would ever have gained the laurel and the crown. To be dependent on others for sympathy and comfort makes you weak; to be self-dependent makes you weaker still, for that fails you in the day of your greatest need; to become independent is a dream of your pride, for no such thing is possible; to become dependent on God makes you strong; yea, clothes you out of his own Almightiness, and draws you up into his safety and refuge.

There is a practice familiarly known in the churches as the "relation of experiences." It is well sometimes, and under proper guards and limits. Indeed, I think with us there is no danger whatever, and that there is too little confluence of heart with heart, and too little conference on the highest themes. But when the whole heart's experience is laid open, we always feel that piety has lost its special grace, and that the finest affections have been soiled by coarse and vulgar handling. As if God had said distinctly, I claim your special confidence. There is a region of experience where no priest shall come between us, where we will tread the wine-press and gain the victory alone. And here precisely is the spot where God fastens on the soul the cords which grapple her closest to his embrace.

In all this course of reasoning, I have considered the argument addressed to those whose experience has not been solely on the surface of things, but has gone somewhat into the deeper mysteries of human nature. That there are natures so cold and so shallow as to have no consciousness of trial so long as the senses are gratified and the course of events which bears them on has had no breaks nor eddies, is certainly true. There are such persons, men and women, who have had no history but the sheerest commonplace story to be read by all men. What we say is, that every one, before he attains the Christian heaven, must be parted off to himself, and what he is spiritually and what he needs must be brought clearly to his individual convictions. There is a realm of being where he must walk alone and gain the victory alone, before he can go up higher. We may lose ourselves in affairs for a while, but the man around whom successful fortune has piled up its ingots, or whom the crowds follow with applause, has a spiritual need within him. And if he does not feel it now, he will with tenfold urgency when this outward show of things has crumbled away like the framework of a dream, and the deeper and more sublime mysteries open clearly into his consciousness. "Do you not see," wrote one on whom had been lavished all the good this outward world can possibly bestow, "that I am dying of melancholy in the height of fortune which once my imagination could scarce have conceived? I have had a high relish for pleasure. I have spent years in intellectual pleasures, but I protest to you that every one of these conditions leaves in the mind a dismal vacuity." There is, indeed, one hidden and consuming woe which some time must prey upon peer and peasant alike, when each comes to himself and stands alone on his rock of independence, with a gulf yawning visibly between himself and his God. It becomes distinct in the consciousness and makes itself audible as earth recedes with its shams and shows. It is the secret sorrow of many a heart too proud to own it to itself, and seeking diversion from itself by the trinkets of human vanity.

Finally, there is one passage of life through which we must pass alike, and in which there is no mortal arm to lean upon, no mortal ear in which to tell the secret of our troubled spirits. "All men," says an eloquent writer, "come into this world alone and leave it alone. Even a child has a dread whispering consciousness, that if he should be called upon to travel into God's presence, no gentle nurse will be allowed to lead him by the hand, no mother to carry him in her arms, no little sister to share his trepidations. King and priest, warrior and maiden, philosopher and child, all must walk these mighty galleries alone. The solitude, therefore, which in this world appalls and fascinates, is but the echo of a far deeper solitude through which he has passed, and of another solitude deeper still, through which he has to pass, — reflex of one solitude, prefiguration of another."

And yet this is rather the appearance of reality than the reality itself; for not alone shall we tread those silent and solemn galleries. We shall enter them alone; but happy is he who, when the curtain rises, shall see on the other side the opening gate in which stands the guiding and beckoning angel.

THE SILENT PRAYER.

STORMS were lowering in the welkin, and the gray clouds
    thicker grew,
And the pine-trees stood as mourners which the winds were
    sobbing through ;

And that night we gathered closer when we heard the east
    wind blow,
"Oh, how cold it must be yonder, sleeping out beneath the
    snow ! "

Friends came in, and close around us stood between us and
    the storm,
And we wept and leaned against them, with their great hearts
    beating warm.

Words, how vain ! but words they spake not, while their
    thoughts rose warm and clear
On their silent prayer-wings upward to the heavenly Father
    near.

Oh, what tones there are in silence, solemn as the toll of
    bells !
Tolling through the heart forever, tolling through its empty
    cells ;

Silence over all the playground, hushing childhood's merry
    glee ;
Silence in the curtained chamber, where the music warbled
    free ;

Silence on the graves out yonder, silence round the empty
   chair ;
But the silence speaketh never like the silence of the prayer.

When some truce from care and sorrow in the arms of sleep
   we found,
Dreaming dreams of little coffins, and a pale face under-
   ground,

Came a glory down the welkin, cleaving darkness like a
   wedge ;
As the sculptor cleaves the marble, cutting clean along the
   edge,

So it cut the solid darkness till it touched the ground below,
Where our little May lay sleeping underneath the winter
   snow ;

And the glory tipped the pine-trees, and I heard the southern
   breeze
Touch them soft as any fingers ever touched the organ keys ;

And a low and rhythmic murmur through the heart this music
   made :
"There is spring without the winter, where the May-flowers
   never fade."

Thrice and four times came the music like a distant travelled
   song,
Coming nearer, nearer, nearer, growing clear and growing
   strong ;

First in sweetly plaintive whispers, like a breeze o'er aspho-
   dels,
Breaking thence in broad effulgence, like the music blown
   from shells.

Then it waked me. Was it only some chance vision of the night?
Or the angel softly muffled lest his garments shine too bright?

Do not all the highest tokens sent in answer to our prayers,
Come along some curtained passage down the bright and heavenly stairs?

I know nothing. Years have vanished since that night of wintry storm,
When the silent prayer went upward from those great hearts beating warm;

But the answer soundeth ever o'er the graves beneath the snow, —
THERE IS SPRING WITHOUT THE WINTER, WHERE THE MAY-FLOWERS ALWAYS BLOW.

IX.

THE NEW CREATION.

2 CORINTHIANS v. 17. *If any man be in Christ, he is a new creature; old things are passed away; behold, all things are become new.*

So early as the middle of the second century we find that works were written against Christianity by heathen philosophers, and written, too, with great subtlety and skill. The keenest of these writers makes it one of his sharpest points of objection that the Gospel professes to accomplish impossibilities; that the idea of changing *human nature* and making it over is utterly absurd. To this the Christian apologists replied: Come and see for yourselves; come into our assemblies and see what and who we are, and from what ranks and conditions we have been gathered. They even affirm that men clean gone down in corruption, and so far gone that the body was gone also — insane people, demoniacs, cripples, blind men, were restored every day; the Spirit operating from within calming, healing, and cleansing at the name of Jesus, and sending health through the whole moral and physical frame. Two things appear constantly in these early histories,— the depth into which human nature had sunk, and the power of Christianity, not to develop it, but to lift it up and create it anew. Indeed, the history of the Church for two hundred years seems a continuation of the book of Acts, and it demonstrates beyond all cavil that the Gospel was not a normal product of human wisdom, but a projection into human affairs out of God's sovereignty, out of the fullness of the Godhead dwelling in Christ.

The power of the Gospel to create anew has been its standing miracle in all the Christian ages. It is its highest and most divine authentication. Celsus was right, looking from his own point of view. No mere human culture can change the *nature* of man. It can only cover over, civilize, and adorn. But those in whom sin has become a second nature are the very persons in whom the Gospel has wrought its most wondrous transformations, from Paul and Augustine down to the Wesleyan revivals of the last century, and the most remarkable conversions of to-day.

In the progress of the Christian ages a great many sects have arisen with controversies without end. But in all sects, and under all forms of belief, so far as the Gospel has done its work, it has been one and the same ; the miracles which began in Palestine continued down all the centuries, changing not the morals and manners only, but the very nature of sinful men. The Gospel may be obscured;

men may eliminate its vital truths, and put their own notions in their place, but so far as it *is* the Gospel it works the old miracles over again. Measures may differ; Christian forms may differ. The revival system may be worked here, and a more staid liturgical system may be worked there; men, according to taste and education, may run into Methodism here, into High Church there, into Broad Church somewhere else; the real Christian work is one and the same — to bring out of the chaos of human nature a new creation in Christ Jesus — and anything that fails of this has not Christ in it, and is not the Gospel.

But let me shape the argument to some practical purpose. Here we are, a minister and people, journeying on through the Christian pilgrimage. Some of us ought to look after the evidences of this great renewal. Let me try to exhibit some of them. They come not by observation. They are not found where often they are looked for most. They are found in the silent individual consciousness, and there they must be sought for if at all. I discriminate, then, change of nature from change of culture and manners, and show what must be the evidence of the new creation in Christ Jesus.

I. The first and most obvious result is *an increase of vital power*. When men become Christians, not in form but in spirit, they have more manhood and womanhood than before. Not the quality only, but the quantity of being is amazingly increased. Of this you have a familiar illustration in the Apostles themselves. While they only knew Christ after the flesh, although He walked among them, how slow of apprehension, how timid and halting in their discipleship, how always on the lookout for themselves, and always trembling for consequences! How totally changed after the spirit of the risen Christ breathed through them, opening wide their perceptions, stirring up all their faculties, giving them breadth, and depth, and freedom, and tongues of flame! Henceforth the hard scales of Judaism fall away from them, and they are new men as if their very identity had been changed. Peter, who denied his Lord at the mock-trial, appears foremost at the Pentecostal scene, and interprets the new phenomena with an insight never had before, and with a tongue loosed from the thraldom of fear. Paul goes towards Damascus a persecuting Jew; he comes from Damascus the apostle of a broad catholicity by which the shell of Judaism was to be shattered in pieces. Then he was full of hate and revenge; now the heart brims over with tender love.

So it has been since the days of Paul, where Christ has been known not after the flesh but after the spirit. Down though the first three centuries, young men, and even boys and girls at the age of fifteen, are described as passing through the ordeals of trial and death with a greatness of heart and a quickness and wisdom of reply, that amazed the stoic philosophers; and yet these had been lifted right up from the besotted influence of pagan idolatry. How and why this is, we shall no longer marvel when we consider that when the Holy Spirit quickens the faculties, it gives them freedom and enlargement. It takes the soul out of its limitations, and sets it face to face with eternal things, and makes it familiar with universal truths and gigantic conceptions. It makes the soul free of the fear of man and the fear of consequences, — fills it with great ideas and warms it with celestial fire.

Have you never observed how insensate men, who were slow of apprehension and slow of speech, have had their whole being replenished and enriched, when Christian truth has fairly taken hold of them, and a Christian experience has roused and enlarged the faculties? How quick and profound afterwards are the souls' intuitions, and how tongues of flame are given them! How easily they break through the mere letter to the spirit within, and grasp warmly the essential truths which the understanding had plodded and groped after in vain! The quantity of being is vastly multiplied, for height, and depth, and breadth are given to its range.

II. The next evidence of this new creation will be found in *the quality of being*, — in the style of thought and imagination. The behavior can be conformed to the best conventional rules. But there the rules stop. They cannot reach the thoughts and imaginations of the mind. And yet, if these are not changed, I need not argue that there is no change of nature within. Will you say that no change is needed here, — no matter what a man thinks, if he only keep it to himself? Remember that out of the heart proceed evil thoughts, adulteries, blasphemies, and murders. And is it enough that their spirit and quality have been so concealed as not to disturb the vibrations of the natural air? Cicero said that if men acted out their dreams they would be insane. He need not have talked of dreams, but only the thoughts and plans and imaginations of waking hours. What would be the sphere of many a goodly company if all the secret thoughts as they arise were projected and laid on the canvas as living pictures, and each saw his own mind out of himself? For under the finest courtesies there may be the foulest spirit-drawing; thoughts running on the line of foul desire; on circumventing the rival who stands in the way; wishes that dare not come to the tongue, or ripen into purposes of action. And because all this unchanged realm of the spirit lies close upon the practical, the practical is so often disturbed. Human nature is not changed unless the realm of thought be made clean; so that even if our thoughts took shape around us upon the air as fast as they come, they would rise on white and unspotted wings. I know very well that this change is not instantaneous in any one; that long after conversion, the style and cast of mind have much of the old habit left; that the Christian must drive off troops of evil suggestions every day. But as fast as our nature does change, our style of thought changes too; and when we are really new creatures in Christ, we are prepared for this inner realm to be laid open as it must be in the judgment time. Then no evil can come into the mind, for its furniture is made pure and sweet like the imagery of an angel's dream. The Christian who really has this great renewal going on within him, finds the need to be less and less for control and watch over all the spontaneous motions of his nature. The man who is not regenerating finds the need to be greater and greater of outward restraints; and age, if it come, will not be the snow crown of heavenly purity and grace, but the breaking down of guards and restraints, that what the man *is* may come more freely into the light of day.

III. Observe now a third indication. Where there is a change of nature, there is a *change of the affections*. We can change our manners, our style of speech and action. But no human power can change the heart. We can disguise it, cover over its propensities, balance them, hold them in, but their intrinsic quality we cannot alter any more than we can alter the constitution of things.

And perhaps you will say there is no need of

changing them. What is purer than infant love? What is sweeter than a child's affections? I answer, they are very sweet and pure, but there is something else in the child waiting development. There is stored up in the heart of every human being, man, woman, or child, what a living writer has aptly termed "latent angers." They are moods and dispositions that come not into our conscious being till we are placed amid the rivalries and temptations of after-life. Sometimes they make their appearance as the spontaneous evolution of a native depravity. The boy has moods which no one provoked, and he sometimes selects a smaller boy as the object of their demonstration. The same demonstrations from our uncleansed human nature we witness in the business and competitions of the world. Business goes wrong and the crosses and rivalries have stirred up the latent angers which should have excited rather magnanimity and quickened the sense of honor and justice; and these dark moods bring a chilling atmosphere into the house or glut their revenge in cruelty to animals,— the innocent creatures who cannot tell the long tale of their oppressions and wrongs. The slaver sees his human property turned into manhood; he cannot destroy the government that wrought the change, so he turns upon the freedmen to persecute and destroy them. There is nothing meaner this side the bottomless pit than these latent angers in manifestation. They generally select the weak on which to expend themselves, and they give the fullest scope to what Macaulay describes, — "the faculty of hating without a provocation." It is some devil of malice that seeks to be gratified with the least of danger, and therefore finds its objects among the hidden relations of human life. It is the unhappiness of an unregenerate nature, and it would make some one else unhappy by way of revenge.

When the child who inherits this evil grows up he will change his method; but if unchanged himself, he keeps his disposition. If he sees those around him more happy than himself, or richer than himself, he will find some way to project his darker mood into their sunshine. And this he will do by disparaging the virtues, or studying to find spots in the characters of other men. Or, very likely, these latent angers will take another form, and if a man has some private pique to be gratified, he will try to revenge it upon the parish or upon the community.

Now the affections are not changed till all this poison has been purged out of them, and these latent angers have not only been denied, but ceased to be; till the heart is a spontaneous fountain of good-will, and leaps up at everybody's joy. Evil moods are shadows projected into us from the pit. If we act from them we fix them there, and sit down in their dismal shade. Resist them and look up, and they retire before the Divine presence till we emerge out of the shadows, and the Christ diffuses sweetness through all the fountains of the heart; and then how easy it is, as Goethe says, "to love God and every little child," — and all the grades between!

IV. Let me describe a fourth indication of change of nature. You know that when the sun has just risen, and for a good while into the forenoon, there are long shadows flung towards the west and towards the north, so that a great many spots are not warmed and blessed with his beams. The western side and the northern side of things remain cold, and the plants and pansies will not start and grow there; and spring is much longer in coming and getting fairly installed in these shadowy places. But when the sun gets up to high noon, or when summer gets to its solstice, all the little corners and northern coverts are reached and quickened; and Nature shoots her shuttles through all these byplaces, and weaves over them her carpet of green. Just so it is with us in the regenerate life. When we begin it, and Christ only slants his beams over us, there are some provinces of duty which we bravely fill, while others are left in the shadows. Some of life's relations are pervaded with the love of God; others have not been thrilled with it at all.

I may be a good neighbor, but not faithful to Christ's Church and cause. Many persons do well enough in their town and neighborhood, who never do aught for the cause of Christianity, which alone makes a neighborhood fit to live in. I may be zealous for religion, but not for humanity, or I may be sunny and sweet as summer to personal friends, but to nobody else. I may be a good Christian sometimes, and then relapse into heathenism, and so my Christian life be fragmentary and incomplete. Only when our sun of righteousness rises toward high noon, does every province of life and duty become warm with it, and the summer green pervades the by-places, where the frosts and the shadows had kept before. And then we know the meaning of the words: "He that is faithful in the least is faithful also in much, and he that is unjust in the least is unjust also in much."

I have named four indications of the new creation, — new vital power; new style of spontaneous thought; new affections purged of latent angers, and all the provinces of duty pervaded and warmed by the noontide. Culture cannot do this. Education cannot do it. A one-sided Christianity, with the moving power of the Gospel left out, cannot do it. Christianity, full-orbed and unobscured always has done this, and always can. If it is not doing it for us, it is because we have not drawn upon its Almighty resources. But no truth regenerates and saves till it is self-applied; when it is self-applied the change begins which is not complete till "old things are passed away and all things are become new."

THE NEW MORNING.

Long had the tears of penitence
  From sleepless eyes been falling,
Long had I heard the still small voice
  That through the soul kept calling;
One night I watched the shapeless clouds
  That o'er my mind were rolling,
Till the clock's slow and solemn tongue
  The hour of twelve was tolling.

Then o'er the loved disciples' page
  Was I my vigils keeping;
I read and prayed, and read again,
  While all the rest were sleeping;
And as I prayed there came a fire,
  Within me gently glowing, —
A calm as when the drooping gales
  At hush of eve stop blowing.

The clouds that o'er my spirit hung
  Then gave a bright forewarning;
They changed to white and purpling flakes
  As at the break of morning.
And then looked through the countenance,
  Clothed in its sun-bright splendor,
Of Him who o'er his Church of old
  Kept holy watch and tender,

His robe was white as flakes of snow
  When through the air descending —
I saw the clouds before him melt,
  And rainbows o'er Him bending;
And then a voice — no, not a voice —
  An inward calm revealing,
Came softly as the steps of Dawn
  O'er tranquil waters stealing.

And ever since, that countenance
  Is on my pathway shining, —
A Sun from out a higher sky
  Whose Light knows no declining:
All day it falls upon my road
  And keeps my feet from straying,
And when at night I lay me down,
  I fall asleep while praying.

X.

CONCERNING DEATH.

(A SERMON ADDRESSED TO CHILDREN.)

AMOS v. 8. *Seek Him who turneth the shadow of death into the morning.*

CHILDREN sometimes have no interest in the sermon because they cannot understand it. There are indeed subjects of great importance which cannot very well be brought home to these youngest hearers. But there are others which they can understand, and about which their young hearts beat with hopes and fears and anxieties. One of these subjects is death, for there are more persons who die in infancy and childhood than at any other age. I know that your hearts are full of that subject this morning, and that I shall be sure of your attention if I adopt a simple style of speech and illustration. And I hope none the less to interest all classes and ages, for there are truths which lose nothing in being clothed in the simplest language, and in learning which we all of us are children before God.

It is a great misfortune, especially in childhood, to get a wrong impression about death; for when that is so, your young day becomes haunted with vague and needless terrors, and you do not prepare for death or for life with intelligence and cheerfulness. I remember my own experience, and how the thought of death rested upon my childhood like a dark and heavy cloud that chilled its innocent joys. It is from a desire of saving you in part at least from a similar experience, that I address you upon this subject. And in order to understand it we will try, in the first place, to remove out of our way some false notions about it. So the sermon will have two parts.

First, we will clear away some mistakes about death; and then show what it really is.

I. First, there is the false idea which we must leave behind, that death is a dark or a lonely passage from this to another world. People get this idea from figurative language found in hymns, in the Bible, and in sermons, and which is understood too literally. You read of "death's cold flood," of "the dark river," and of "the valley of the shadow of death." Of course it cannot be a valley and a river both. Figures of speech are addressed to the feelings and the imagination. They are images to represent realities, not the realities themselves. But the figure in this case has often been taken for the fact itself, not only by children but by older persons. But when so taken it gives you a totally wrong impression; for in dying you will neither go over a river, or through a valley, nor go anywhere, as we shall see when we come to unfold the subject.

Let us clear away another delusion. You would sometimes infer from what you read in books or hear in sermons, that death will bring you into the awful presence of God, such as will overwhelm or terrify. You hear of "the bar of God," and "the judgment-seat," as if death were a summons to some dread tribunal with a stern Almighty Judge sitting upon it. Now we know very well, both from the Bible and from the nature of the case, that this cannot be in any literal sense of the word. The only way to see God is by becoming pure and good, and if you are not pure and good you will no more see God in another world than you will in this. We approach God by becoming more like Him. He is near to us in Christ when we are Christ-like. We become conscious of his presence through Christian progress and regeneration. Hence we read, "Blessed are the pure in heart for they shall see God." Merely dying will not cause us to see God any more than a change of garments will do it, unless after death we shall advance more rapidly in the heavenly life. And then to see God will be our highest bliss. It will make us glad and joyous like seeing the sun and rejoicing in his beams. The punishment of the wicked is that they cannot see God, but are away from Him. It is his absence that we have most to dread. To be without God in this world, or in any other, is the supreme desolation. It is being brought near Him that we have most to desire, as is expressed in the hymn you sing sometimes, —

"Nearer, my God, to thee — nearer to thee."

Let us clear away another delusion. We get an impression about death such as the heathen had, that it destroys the most real and substantial part of us and turns us into ghosts. Hence the belief in spectres ; and hence the notion that ghosts cannot be completely happy till they come back into the same body again, — a notion which the Jews brought from Babylon, and hence it comes into our Christian literature. So you read on tombstones sometimes, "This dust shall rise again." I should be sorry to think so ; sorry to believe that when the body falls away from us we are less real and substantial beings, and not rather more so ; sorry to think that this world of dull sense and matter, beautiful as it is, is the best world that God has made ; sorry to think that these bodies of flesh and blood are the best bodies which God creates. Let us dismiss, then, this notion of ghostly existence after death, and think of it as the very fullness of warm and positive being, throbbing and blooming with a life which the pulses of these mortal bodies are too languid to measure. Hence, in all the Scripture scenes which give us gleams of the immortal life, they picture it to us not as more dim and shadowy, but as more bright and real, — as in the transfiguration scene where Moses and Elijah appeared in glory.

Sleep is another false image under which death is described to us. This, too, was borrowed from the heathen; but how largely has it entered into Christian literature and affected our modes of thinking and speaking. People call it sleep because it appears so to the senses, forgetting that sometimes these appearances are the very opposite of reality. "Asleep in Jesus," I have read as the epitaph of a good man, when the sleepiest of all people are those who fall away from Jesus, and those who are really in Him are kept widest awake.

Clearing off this false imagery, we are prepared for the positive and glorious truth to which we are now coming. We have seen what death is not and what it will not do. Let us now see what it is and what it will do.

Before I come to show what it is, perhaps I ought to answer a question which you will naturally ask me. How do I know anything about it? How can any one know about it who has never died? Let me answer by saying, I suppose we know as much about it as we ever shall or ever can. We shall not know any more about dying by going through the process of death, for the simple reason that in the process itself it annihilates all sensation. A great many persons have experienced everything up to the point where sensation ceases, and then come back to life and told us their whole experience. More than this, the Bible tells us of some who passed beyond that point and opened their eyes upon the after scene and then came back and told us all about it. Christ was an instance of this kind. St. John was another — similar, though not the same. After death we shall know more of what is beyond; we shall not know more of the fact itself for the simple reason that we shall not be conscious of it. We learn what death is from the Divine revelations and from the nature of the case.

II. *Death is waking up out of sleep.* It is not sleep itself, but just the opposite, waking up out of sleep. Those few words probably describe it as perfectly as any words can. I suppose, my young hearers, you experience something exactly analogous to death every morning. During the night your senses are locked fast in sleep. Still you are not unconscious. You see things in your dreams, but you see them dimly. You work and play, and wander over fields, and go to see friends and friends come to see you; all the while shut in to that dream-land which you explore at will. In that dream-world you have your griefs and pleasures, trials and joys. But there is another world all around you which for the time you do not see. Perhaps the morning sun rises and shines through the windows and finds you sleeping still, living in that world of dreams and shadows. There is a bright sky over you, and the green earth all around you, and the morning air is broken into whirls and eddies of song from a thousand birds, but you see and hear nothing of all this, for sleep has locked you fast in that land of dreams. Good dreams they may be, giving you the images and impressions of the waking world; but they are not that waking world itself, only its image and representation. But by and by your senses unclose, the dream-world all vanishes, and lo! this other world of sky and earth, and woods and waters, is all given to your sight. How have you passed from that world of shadows into this real world of beauty and song? By going away somewhere? No, but by waking up. You open your eyes and pass from one world into another — not by travelling, but simply by the exercise of another set of faculties which have waked into consciousness. But please to understand that you have not yet waked into the highest world. There is a brighter one yet, compared with which all this outward scene is a land of dreams and shadows. What you saw in your sleep compared with what you saw when you awoke, is as this world we now look upon compared with the one we shall see when death wakes us to a sight of its realities. We are in it now, though we sleep and dream and therefore do not see it. Hence we find that good books call this a dream, and this world a fleeting show. As in those lines, —

> "This life is but a fleeting show,
> For man's illusion given."

Or, as the Psalmist has it, "Every man walketh in a

vain show," or, as some render, "among empty shadows." They only mean that this outward life, with all its shows, is unreal and dim compared with the one which we wake into at the touch of death. "The fashion of this world passeth away," says an Apostle. We shut our eyes on it at death and wake up in another, just as we wake from our night dreams into the midst of bright realities every morning. So friends, when they die, do not travel off into space to find the spiritual world. They have a sense within which simply wakes up to what before was all around and within them, though invisible. You have souls within you. These souls are the immortal and substantial part of you, though, alas! they are now comparatively asleep, and at best only dream and imagine what shall be hereafter. The soul is the real man, having its own class of faculties, though closed and locked in a mortal body. Death is simply the waking up of those faculties to the bright and embracing world of immortality.

And I do not know that death will be our last waking. I do not know but we may have deeper senses yet, which death now may not touch and open. Perhaps we have ranges of faculties, one within another, each with its own world and modes of being, so that we may keep waking up, stage after stage, to brighter realms, for ever and ever away towards God, the central life and glory of all. I will not dogmatize; but who shall say that we may not to all eternity, at some of its stages, die to a more outward life and wake up to a more inward and real one? that after we have lived out the life of one world faithfully, a new one will open more brightly and objectively, where there is a higher order of existence, and God reveals Himself in diviner splendor — all coming from the successive waking up into intenser life of faculties that sleep already within us? Be that as it may, let us lay it up as a first truth, Death is not a sleep, but a waking. This is our sleep; our dull life in these sluggish bodies. Death wakes us out of this, and then it is morning.

In all that I have now said, I have considered myself as describing death as it is to good men and innocent children. I do not mean to say that it will wake every one immediately into a higher and brighter scene. But it will wake each one to see just the world he is already in and belongs to. It is a great mistake to think that God will raise men to heaven or send them to dismal abodes, merely because they die. Can we not grasp this great truth, that men go to a good world or a bad one before they die, and that death only touches them to wake them up, and show them where they are? Attend one moment and we can make this plain.

Here is a man who is sleeping in a pleasant garden, embowered in fragrant shades and blooming roses. Friends may be walking all around him, and watching his slumber, and birds of paradise may fling golden shadows over him from their wings. But he does not see all this. He is locked in his own world and only dreaming of it. He is asleep. By and by some friend comes and touches him, and says, "Sleep no longer! wake to what is about you!" He does wake, and by the very act of waking becomes cognizant of all those pleasant things. He has not gone away somewhere to find them. He was among them before, and only waked up to see them. So it is with good men and good children. They are in heaven before they die in heart and spirit; with God and his Christ and his angels, for these draw around the good man, — encamp round about him, as the Psalmist says, and death only wakes him, that he may find himself among the sweet societies. Death comes to such as an angel friend — as if he would say as he touches them, "Sleep no more! wake up from those earth dreams to these blessed realities."

But again, there is a man asleep amid scenery very different from this; in some den of wretchedness, among evil companions, and perhaps angry words and blasphemies grate on his sleeping ear. He, too, is shut in to his dream-world.

Troubled dreams they are which now disturb him, and in his sleep he wanders amid no green and grateful scenery. Where will he be when he awakes? Just where he had placed himself. Amid evil companions, and in wretched abodes. He has waked up amid just the society which he covets and loves, and to just such pleasures as he is fitted to enjoy. He has not travelled away to find them. He was there before. Even so let us remember that bad men, before they die, have withdrawn from the communion of God and heaven and angels. They have travelled away from these already, and death only wakes them up to where they are — the evil companionship which they love, and the dismal surroundings which it creates. Bear away, then, this momentous truth, that good deeds and pure affections make heaven; yea, that by these you travel into it, and death merely opens your eyes to its scenery; that evil dispositions and evil passions make hell; yea, that by these you travel into it now, and death only opens your eyes to its scenery.

I trust I have shown you plain enough, that death merely is not to be feared, but that the only momentous question is, where death will find you. We dismiss the notion that after death we are to travel off somewhere through dreary spaces, and stop somewhere in unknown worlds. Our spiritual travelling is done before death. It is change of state, not change of place. What a blessed thought! — that we are not to cross streams and dark valleys to find the happy abodes and peaceful homes, but that we may wake to higher life and find ourselves among the shining ones, just as we wake out of a dream in the morning and find ourselves in our homes and families. But in order to do this, we must be of the same temper, spirit, and purpose. There is no such thing as *going* to heaven ; but you may become heavenly-minded, and then death will wake you out of the more sluggish existence of earth, to the more visible realities of a heavenly world.

And how, you will ask, are we to become heavenly-minded ? I have already implied how this may be. But to make it very plain, I present it in two points which you can remember and carry away.

First, we become heavenly-minded by living to make others happy. That includes almost the whole. The employments of heaven, as we read, consist in making others happy. That is what is meant by the word angel. It is a messenger, and a messenger of good, sent to bestow blessings. When we live to bless others we become like them, messengers of good. If the employments of earth only had this end in view, heaven would be brought down into all its affairs. If it is the aim and work of your life to be a blessing to others, you are living already the heavenly life, and you will be only more openly and visibly in heaven when death wakes you to its scenery and surroundings.

But we cannot make others happy except we are good ourselves. And we cannot be good ourselves except as God makes us so by our communings with Him, as He is revealed in his Christ, and thence seeks to form his own image both in men and in little children. I present in these two points the pith and essence of a great many sermons and even whole libraries. Live to make others happy and heaven is already entered; and in order to this, "Seek Him who turneth the shadow of death into the morning."

The fact which I stated at the beginning of my sermon, is a very interesting one: that nearly half of those who die are children. In one view this depresses and saddens us, for it is so much of God's beautiful flock taken from the homes and pleasant haunts of earth. But when we remember that all this young life is flowing into the heavens and helps to keep them fresh and strong, the idea is forced upon us that children are needed there as well as here, and that the homes of heaven, like those of earth, are not full without them. We should not murmur, then, when called upon to "halve the lot" with those above us.

> "To us, these graves; to them, the rows
>   The mystic palm-trees spring in.
> To us, the silence in the house;
>   To them, the choral singing."

LITTLE WILLIE WAKING UP.

SOME have thought that in the dawning,
  In our being's freshest glow,
God is nearer little children
  Than their parents ever know,
And that if you listen sharply,
  Better things than you can teach,
And a sort of mystic wisdom
  Trickles through their careless speech.

How it is, I cannot answer,
  But I knew a little child
Who among the thyme and clover
  And the bees was running wild;
And he came one summer evening,
  With his ringlets o'er his eyes,
And his hat was torn in pieces
  Chasing bees and butterflies.

"Now I'll go to bed, dear mother,
  For I'm very tired of play!"
And he said his "Now I lay me"
  In a kind of careless way;
And he drank the cooling water
  From his little silver cup,
And said gayly, "When it's morning,
  May the angels take me up!"

Down he sank with roguish laughter
  In his little trundle bed,

And the kindly god of slumber
  Showered poppies o'er his head.
"What could mean his speaking strangely?"
  Asked his musing mother then,
"Oh 'twas nothing but his prattle,—
  What could he of angels ken?

"There he lies, how sweet and placid!
  And his breathing comes and goes
Like a zephyr moving softly,
  And his cheek is like a rose;
But his mother leaned to listen
  If his breathing could be heard;
"Oh," she murmured, "if the angels
  Took my darling at his word!"

Night within its folding mantle
  Has the sleepers both beguiled,
And within its soft embracings
  Rest the mother and the child;
Up she starteth from her dreaming,
  For a sound has struck her ear,
And it comes from little Willie
  Lying on his trundle near.

Up she springeth, for it striketh
  On her troubled ear again,
And his breath in louder fetches
  Travels from his lungs in pain;
And his eyes are fixing upward
  On some face beyond the room,
And the blackness of the spoiler,
  From his cheek has chased the bloom.

Never more his "Now I lay me"
  Will be said from mother's knee;
Never more among the clover
  Will he chase the humble-bee;
Through the night she watched her darling,
  Now despairing, now in hope,
And about the break of morning
  Did the angels take him up.

XI.

THE UNIVERSAL REDEMPTION.

ROMANS viii. 19-21. *The earnest expectation of the creature waiteth for the manifestation of the sons of God. For the creature was made subject to vanity, not willingly, but by reason of Him who hath subjected the same in hope; because the creature itself also shall be delivered from the bondage of corruption, into the glorious liberty of the children of God.*

I DO not know of anything out of the sayings of Jesus that describes with such power and unction the renewing energy of the Gospel, as this eighth chapter to the Romans. We shall not get the full scope of Paul's doctrine, however, without a little verbal explanation and criticism. This word "creature" does not mean man exclusively; at least I can give it no such narrow interpretation. It includes all animal existence as well; all the dumb natures below man who are subject to him as the lord of the earth, "having dominion over the fish of the sea and over the fowl of the air and over every living thing that moveth upon the earth." And the meaning of the word extends yet farther, and includes insensate and inanimate things; for the writer says by a bold personification, "the whole creation" groaneth and travaileth in pain and yearns for its deliverance. When we remember Paul's Rabbinical learning and style of conception, we cannot doubt that this is his thought; that he sees inanimate nature as it were in sympathy with man, as if the taint of his corruption had run down into the lowest things and was also to be purged away from them, so that in the times of the Messiah there shall be a new earth for the abode of righteousness. He hears the undertones of all nature moaning for her deliverance from the dominion of sin. Man and animal and inanimate nature I understand to be all included under the phrase, "the whole creation" which groaneth and travaileth in pain.

They are all made subject to "vanity," says the Apostle, not by their own will but through the will of the Creator. But this word "vanity," is very inadequate to give his idea. He describes the same in the verse following as "the bondage of corruption." He means plainly evil in general with all its attendant sufferings, which, beginning in the nature of man, involves all natures below him so that when man shall be delivered from it, the whole creation will also rejoice in the deliverance and enjoy "the glorious liberty of the children of God."

All this may seem visionary. Doubtless it is visionary; for all prophecy comes from vision, albeit it is vision which one day is to become reality. Let us see then in what way these splendid ideals which filled the Apostle's field of view are to become realities through the power of the Christian Gospel. The Christian redemption takes its course downward, reaching man first and then all natures below him. Let us follow its course in this direction.

I. "We who have the first-fruits of the Spirit wait for the adoption, namely, "the redemption of our body." The redemption of our body from what? Why from these lusts and passions which make it the servant of sin and draw it down and away from the service of the soul. Our body does not mean here merely our material coverings but the whole outward man which bodies forth the spiritual nature within, and which is the receptacle of all our inherited depravities. This is the bondage of corruption which holds the soul in thraldom, and out of which the soul sighs for deliverance. Paul terms it in another connection "the body of death," where he describes man as it were split in two and striving in opposite directions; as if the individual in his double consciousness were resolved into two men, one delighting supremely in the law of God, the other urging into captivity to the law of sin which is in "our members." In our modern phraseology we call these two the higher and the lower nature,— the former receptive of the Holy Spirit and answering to its call, the other the abode of all our stormful and unclean passions and responding to the sorceries of the tempter. This outward or natural man, called the body of sin, is not made up of flesh and blood merely ; for flesh and blood may drop away altogether and still the spiritual body be the abode of depraved passions and appetites. These material coverings which we wear obey the law of the immortal man within them ; let that be purged of evil and it will transform the whole outward nature and make our material clothings fit to us as our robe of righteousness. In its changes and transformations it shall become obsequious to the soul that "delights in the law of God after the inward man." Matter is neither good nor evil except as magnetized by the spirit within ; and though the natural man may not become free at once from all taint of corruption hereditary or acquired, perhaps never in this life, yet the full power of the Christian Gospel shall bring the whole gang of passions and appetites into complete quiescence, so that the motions of the regenerate heart, love, mercy, compassion, charity, and goodwill shall have their forthgoing without hindrance, and then the redemption of our body is complete.

Among all the vices gendered in this "body of sin," cruelty, perhaps, is the worst and the most devilish. It would be unjust to the animal to say without qualification that cruelty makes men brutal, for there are brutes that are not cruel, but gentle and harmless, and which have a sort of sympathy with the sufferings of others. Cruelty allies men with the lowest and most savage natures of the animal kingdom, its wolves, its tigers, and its serpents. And neither science nor civilization have sovereign power to soften or subdue its spirit. On the other hand, they only make its weapons more polished and keen and withal more destructive. They change the war-club first for the spear and the sword, and then for shot and shell. And what a spectacle has the world presented of the many in subjection to the few! the human wolves and tigers on the kingly and priestly thrones; the multitudes driven into slaughter-pens as if they were so many herds of animals to be extinguished without remorse. Good heavens! we exclaim, as we follow the track of history; is this the story of our race or of some other; were these men and women who could feel and sympathize and reason and suffer, or were they the monsters of a geologic age before the earth had become green, and before the sun had begun fairly to shine? But they were the material which Christianity had to work upon; they were the people from which we have descended, and the first achievement of Christianity was to rescue the many from the cruelties of the few, that the human creation need no longer travail in pain for its deliverance.

II. But the animal creation needed deliverance as much and even more; for these are dumb natures that could not tell their wrongs, and have no power to redress them. The animals had no rights which men considered themselves bound to respect. And yet the susceptibility to suffering of the more sensitive animals is equal to, and even greater, than that of many human beings. They are capable, not only of bodily suffering, but suffering from fear, terror, grief, anguish, and the baffled yearnings of those instincts which are the endowments of all animal natures. They are capable, too, of being brought into such sympathy with man as to reflect back upon him, not only the kindness and affection of his nature, but also some flashes of his reason and intelligence. How desolate the earth would be without them! How vacant the air if they did not winnow it with their wings and turn it into songs and serenades! What a solitude were the woods and the groves unless they were made alive with these natives that fill them with the signs of delight and joy, and with the exquisite grace of form and motion, and sometimes with melodies more sweet than the music we hear in churches! And what a helpless being were civilized man, unless "every living thing that moveth on the earth" were brought into his service and made obedient to his will! Through the air, the earth, and the sea, the Creator has poured these streams of conscious life, in order that the whole universe down even through its smallest veins shall throb with happiness and joy. If He had not created them for enjoyment, would He have organized them so finely and sent nerves of feeling all through them to thrill with pleasure ; would He have made the gambols of the squirrel exhilarating as the play of children upon the village green ; would He have made the linnet to delight in the gushes of his own song ; would He have given instinct to the dog mighty as our human affection, whose disappointment is so cruel that he dies of bereavement ; would He have put such meaning into the appealing eye and voice of the horse and the kine, and such a tongue in their groans and agonies ; would He have secreted in the eye-vessels of the deer those little reservoirs of water, to roll down his cheeks in great tear-drops of anguish when hunted and wounded by ruthless men ? Oh, if these creatures over which man has dominion had a language in which to send up their petitions and publish their oppressions and wrongs, it would fill quite as large a volume, and quite as thick with blood-stains as any book of human oppressions and martyrdoms. And yet the pleadings go up daily to the eternal mercy from this lower creation that groaneth and travaileth in pain together until now!

In the Oriental superstitions there was often an infusion of mercy, and they were permitted because they brought animals and birds, and insects even, into tender sympathy with humanity as if they were a part of it. The doctrine of transmigration taught that human souls had become reincarnate in the bodies of animals, where they were doing penance for their former sins, and so the Brahmin hears from out these animal natures muffled human voices, and sees human eyes, as it were, looking up and pleading for sympathy and protection. It was a heathen superstition with a half truth in it, and this half truth has done in pagan lands what the Christian whole truth should have done long ago in ours; for it should have made the brute creation so far forth partakers in the human redemption as to banish all needless suffering down even to the insect that sports in the morning sunbeam. The wholesale slaughtering warfare which has been made upon them is not less horrible than our wars of race with race and nation with nation, and not less opposed to the millennial reign of peace and good-will on the earth. As long as man "murders their species" he will "betray his own;" for the spirit of murder and treachery enters into him and takes possession and goes out anew to desolate the earth. In the new Christian civilization that is now dawning, many an Agassiz is to arise and plead the cause of those who could only plead for themselves in dumb agonies; is to reveal the nature of these tribes below us; which are the noxious and which are harmless; which are man's allies and helpers and which are not; how death for them as for human beings may be deprived of its sting, and how every needless pang inflicted cries both to God and man for avenging justice. How strange that instead of admiring the exquisite divine workmanship in the wing of the bird a man should lurk in the thicket as an assassin; instead of joining his note to her morning song, should delight only to turn it into a death-note or quench the music of the groves in innocent blood! "New Studies in Natural History!" — it is to be hoped they will be introduced not only into the colleges but into the schools and the nurseries and the Sunday-schools, until all God's innocent creatures shall have protection under Christianity as well as heathenism. For there is a quasi-humanity in these dumb animals. Theodore Parker believed some of them immortal; I trust they are not, for alas! what multitudes of them would rise up in another state to confront their human murderers at the judgment-seat! But then what human qualities are drawn out of them by the power of kindness! What constancy and affection and gratitude that rebuke and shame the selfishness of men! What sympathy with the beauty and grandeur in nature, and sometimes in art even, when what is noble and good is appealed to and brought into manifestation! The horses of the circus will keep step to strains of exhilarating music with a conscious delight, till you begin to wonder which is the more human, the horse or the mountebank that rides upon his back. The long cavalcade moves to martial strains, the animals quite as much as the men, with a pride and a glorying in their eyes and nostrils; their necks "clothed with thunder" and their feet in rhythmic dances, as if one spirit had entered them all and moved them with one purpose and will.

In that day when the savagery in men has been eliminated or softened down, the savagery in brute natures will be softened also as reflecting his own nature back upon him ; for there are fine invisible nerves that pervade all the universe and run down from man into all the lower creation, and when he is himself redeemed will draw the lower creation towards him and harmonize it with him in one great atonement. For in just the measure that the lion in man's nature lies down with the lamb, just in the same measure will the peace be radiated on all things about him. And so to fulfill the old prophecy spiritually will tend in some sort to its fulfilment literally.

"The wolf shall dwell with the lamb,
And the leopard shall lie down with the kid ;
The calf and the young lion and the fatling shall be together,
And a little child shall lead them.
The suckling shall play upon the hole of the asp,
And the new-weaned child lay his hand on the hiding-place of the adder.
They shall not hurt nor destroy in all my holy mountain :
For the land shall be full of the knowledge of the Lord,
As the waters cover the depths of the sea."

III. But will the redemption stop here ? No, it must keep on till all insensate and inanimate things as well are made partakers of it. By a bold personification, as I understand him, the Apostle gives to the earth itself a sort of consciousness of the woes and sufferings on its surface. It is what the old prophets had done before, when they made all nature sympathize with man both in his joys and his sorrows. When man rejoices, "the mountains can break forth into singing and all the trees of the field can clap their hands;" and again the innocent blood can cry from the ground as if the earth kept throwing it up and refused to drink it in. The ear of the prophet seemed to catch the undertones of nature and hear her cry, as if the earth had a voice and said: "O ye children of men, how long will ye turn the treasures which I yield to base and cruel ends! How long will ye rend my bosom to find the enginery of destruction, not of beneficence and mercy! How long will ye dig the mines I hold in trust for you — the gold, the iron, the nitre and the gems — to sate your avarice, cruelty, and pride, and not rather to cover me with the arts and industries of benefice and peace? How long will ye distill the juices of my vineyards and orchards for your drunkenness and revelry? And how long must I receive the bodies of your murdered victims and throw them up again before the heavens that look down as the witnesses against you?" All this, you will say, is figure; but it is not *all* figure. There is a sort of sympathy of all nature with all humanity. She copies out of man what is in him, that he may see himself face to face. And so her types beneficent will grow fairer to us, and sparkle with a more glorious beauty as we grow better and drink more largely the spirit of mercy; and her ugly deformities will grow more ugly if they become the looking-glass of our own mind. Yea, more, every man in some sort creates the world he lives in and makes the sunshine he sees about him, for his own spirit is the prismatic ground from which the light is turned into sweet colorings and reflections of the smile of God ; while again,

> " He who has foul thoughts and a dark soul,
> Benighted walks under the midday sun,
> Himself is the own dungeon."

And what is this world outside of us which we call nature but the changeable vesture which the Creator casts about us ? It is not fixed and dead, but a fresh creation of God every hour. It always has had its adaptations to the beings on its surface, and it always must have. And so man's redemption is at the same time the redemption of all the creatures over which he has dominion, and the redemption of nature from the curse that lay upon it, for the curse is primarily in himself. Let his own mind and heart become paradisical and he will enter paradise again, for its light will be on the fields, the rivers, and the mountains. "Instead of the thorn shall come up the fir-tree, and instead of the brier shall come up the myrtle-tree," and the three kingdoms of earth — man and animal and inanimate nature — be delivered from the bondage of corruption into the glorious liberty of the children of God.

Such is the extent of the gospel redemption ! It moves on steadily and surely. If it has not yet involved you it is because you choose to withstand it and will not put yourself into its plastic hands. For it works not by magic, but by its own laws and methods. The Jesus Christ who met Saul of Tarsus on his way and melted all his cruelties out of him, that he might become the prophet of a Gospel so humane and tender, has the same power over us as over him; is just as near us behind these clouds of sense, and in a power and splendor more warm and bright than the Syrian noon; and only asks of us a childlike surrender to his sovereign creative power, that he may work the same transformation, and change all the native fountains of gall into the milk of kindness.

THE YOUNG HUNTER.[1]

"Come, my boy, and in the meadows
   Tend the little lambs to-day;
Play with them beside the brooklets
   Where they pluck the flowers so gay."
"Mother, mother, with my bow
To the mountains I must go."

"Why not with the horn's brisk music
   Lead the cattle through the dells?
Lovely in the Alpine pastures
   Is the tinkling of the bells."
"On the mountains with my bow,
Mother, mother, let me go."

"Go and tend the flowerets, blooming
   In their garden beds, my child;
In the garden all is pleasant, —
   But the mountain-tops, how wild!"
"Let the flowerets bloom and grow,
Mother, mother, let me go!"

Through the mountain's wildest regions
   The young hunter rushed away,
Where the steep and winding pathway
   Scarcely sees the light of day,
And before the hunter near
Flies the swift gazelle in fear.

[1] A translation from Schiller.

Climbing with a breezy motion,
　On the ribs of rock she clings;
O'er the deeply yawning fissures
　With a lightsome bound she springs;
And the hunter from below,
Follows with his deadly bow.

Now she gains a rocky splinter,
　Hanging from its highest steep;
There she sees the pathway vanish,
　And before the dreadful deep, —
Sees the fatal steep below,
And behind, her cruel foe.

With a look of deepest sorrow
　And beseeching agony,
Turns she toward her cruel hunter,
　Dumbly pleading with her eye;
But regardless of her woe
He levels straight the deadly bow.

Sudden from a rocky fissure
　Rose a form of awful grace;
'T was the Spirit of the Mountain,
　'T was the Genius of the place;
And the quivering gazelle
With his hands he shielded well.

Then he turned upon the hunter
　While his eyes with anger glowed
"Must you carry death and sorrow
　Clear up here to mine abode?
Earth has room for all her own,
Let my beauteous flock alone!"

XII.

THE BOX OF OINTMENT.

MARK xiv. 8. *She hath done what she could.*

BY collating the synoptics with John, we bring before us very distinctly the whole scene. Jesus enters the house of Simon weary with travel, and with his mind filled with images of his approaching death, and this woman comes in with a box of liquid balsam with which she bathes his feet, while with spice-waters she bathes his aching brow. The room is filled with the perfume. Judas reproves the woman for wasting the balsam, while Jesus commends her, and assures the disciples that the fragrance of this deed shall yet fill the whole world.

This woman had seen the miracles of Christ, and heard his heavenly speech, and been persuaded of his Divine character and mission. And then the question naturally arises, What can I do for him? I, — without power, or wealth, or position in the world. I can give nothing but an expression of sympathy and good-will. So she seizes impulsively the costliest thing she had, and lavishes it upon the person of her Lord. It was all she could do. And when Judas rebukes the woman, Jesus rebukes his disciple. " Let her alone. Wherever the Gospel is preached in all time, this deed shall be recounted with it as exhaling its spirit of devoted love." She hath done what she could. Have the most earnest and self-sacrificing among you done any more?

This little piece of biography, however, has come down to us, not merely to immortalize the memory of this humble disciple, but to embody and illustrate forever the doctrine of the Master. For this doctrine is preserved most perfectly in the narratives of the New Testament. You are not sure of the meaning when you get into Paul's metaphysics, who uses the nomenclature of the old Jewish schools; but you never mistake the meaning in these scraps of biography, where the truth lives and breathes, and is fragrant through all time.

The feeling which prompted this deed of personal faith and affection, is one, I suppose, which every Christian heart is sometimes conscious of. What can I do for Christ? How wide and how great is the work to be done, and how little is my share in it!

And there is no person whose religious experience is any way profound, who has not been brought sometimes to a point where the dread account seems to be striking the balance and going down heavily against him; some hour of painful self-analysis, some day when sickness laid you down, and in the stillness of the room your past life seemed to stream over your memory like a flame, and disclose its record, somewhat as it will be disclosed at the judgment-bar. At these times, what is done looks so indescribably poor and meagre, tainted with all manner of imperfection, having all your faults of temper put into it, and all your mistakes of method, that you turn away with loathing, and it is not strange at all that in this state of mind so many have sought for peace in imputed or factitious righteousness. And then, come our failures every day in our efforts to build up a perfect character. Some taint of self is sure to get into it; some invading temptation is sure to assail it, and in one hour lay all the flourishing structure in the dust. And then the old question comes back with tenfold pungency, How shall man be justified before God? It is a very simple question, but it goes so directly to the very substance of the Gospel that it has been the main work of theology to answer it, for eighteen hundred years.

But we will endeavor to grasp the principle which lies at the heart of this beautiful narrative; we must see the Gospel truth embodied there, and which alone has filled the world with the perfume of this woman's deed, and earned the benediction of her Lord.

I. The question so long debated about works, gets here a very definite answer. It is not the amount nor the extent of a man's well-doing, that makes his deeds a fragrant sacrifice unto God. I think the lives of the great saints and great heroes have sometimes a very depressing influence upon us who cannot be great in anything. This woman's life, judged so, were a total failure. But one deed of affection has brought her fully into light, and placed her example aloft to demonstrate wherever the Gospel is preached, that those who do what they can in the humblest and meanest sphere of duty, are equal before God with those who do the most, though they cover the world with blessings. Judged by our achievements there is poor prospect for any of us. Even great men, and famous men, out of their insignificant individualism accomplish little. Judged so, and falling back into their own proper selves, they are weak and puny enough. Only because they are put in representative positions where they are exponents of something beyond themselves, they become great. No mortal man is great in himself; he only becomes so by representing some tract, great or small, of the Divine Providence. Just before the fact related in the text was transpiring, a young man, a boy, you might say, was raised by circumstances to the throne of the Cæsars. He took the title of Great; his glory filled the civilized world, and the age was called by his name. And yet this woman with her box of ointment has made a single deed of personal love to diffuse a wider and sweeter fragrance than all the deeds of Augustus Cæsar. So you see it is not how much we have done, but what we have tried to do, that justifies us before God. He does not need our success to help on his infinite plan. That plan proceeds by our failures as by our triumphs. Both are alike to him, for He takes them both up, transfigures them, and weaves them into his cloth of gold, that makes up the warp and the woof of time. And I am not sure, if we look well at the matter, but we shall find that when the vast fabric has all been woven, the mistakes and weaknesses of men, the blunders and failures, will show as important threads as their most splendid success and victories. Even so the Gethsemanes, the Pharsalias, and the Bull Runs of history, help the Divine plan, along with the Plateas, the Yorktowns, and the Gettysburgs. Look back you who have worked the hardest and the longest, and see how little is the amount when you have summed it all up, and how many a man with larger machinery, by only setting it going and looking on with folded hands, has turned out an aggregate vastly more substantial and magnificent. Works! may the Lord save us! but is it strange at all that orthodoxy has decided that our works, pile them up as we will, cannot do it? for still they are ragged and incomplete, and have no rounding grace in them. Yes,— and when we thought to do the most for the Lord, perchance we are crippled, and all our schemes come to nothing through a weakened sinew, or a disordered nerve, or some rebellious lobe in the brain that refused its function.

If you look through a magnifying glass upon one of the landscape paintings of Titian you will find that the more you magnify the more of ugliness and deformity and imperfection will be revealed in it. If you look through the same magnifying glass upon any of God's works, if it be only a flower, or a snowflake, you will find that the more you magnify the more of beauty and perfection will be revealed. And the reason is this: that man's weakness and limitation enter into the best of his works, and their most exquisite finish and grace lie only on the surface; whereas in God's works, the perfection and the beauty open in endless perspective the more we magnify, where we catch dissolving views of the infinite glory.

God will not say to us, then, when He calls us into judgment, Bring a specimen of your work, and let me see with what finish and completeness you have turned it out. Turn it out as we will it has no round and complete grace, and all our piled up manufactures cannot reach into heaven. No — but there is another test by which He will judge us and by which He judges us now. Not by what we have done, but *by what we have tried to do* shall we be judged, and even our everlasting destiny determined. What we have planned and purposed and tried to execute —

these are the tests — no matter if in the execution we run against walls and barricades every hour. Hell is paved with good intentions, says an old theologian, in this as in other things turning the truth exactly upside down. Heaven is paved with good intentions and with nothing else. "She hath done what she could." Not performances, but endeavors, He asks of us; and if the endeavors be honest and hearty, no matter, as God sees us, how ragged and incomplete the execution. And here we can imitate God and be like Him, having the same end and aim; and herein He works with us and is glorified in us, — taking up our poor performance and weaving it into the woof of his infinite providence.

And so we find that the poor woman who put three mites into the treasury since it was one hundred per cent. of her income, and the Mary who balmed his head with balsam odors, since it was all she could do, are the equals of him who girdles the globe with charities, since, though not alike in what they have done, they are alike in what they have tried to do.

So this box of perfume has not only preserved this woman's deed and diffused its savor over Christendom — it has brought down and preserved with it this principle of gospel justification, that not by the grand total of your success, but by your strivings after it, you are to be judged at the bar of God and obtain his benediction of Well done.

II. So much about works. But this is not all. What the faith is that saves us comes out with equal clearness. Do you suppose this woman could have made a statement of her theology that the synods and councils would have accepted? And yet here is faith most wonderful and abounding — faith in the sense of confiding and trusting, such confiding as made one give up the costliest thing she had, and waste it in the lavishment of affection.

If there is anything which the New Testament makes clear beyond all cavil, it is that no amount of statement and definition constitutes that faith in Christ, which justifies and saves. Not by any means, however, would we deny that our conception of the Gospel may be very usefully defined and formulated so that we can handle it and teach it, and carry it about in distinct propositions, and have resting-places for the intellect. But formulate it as we will, we are still to remember, that our richest, tenderest experiences of its adorable mercy elude our statements and lose their flavor in our words. That, indeed, is the mystic meaning of the odors of this sacred balm. They mean the ineffable love with which all saving faith is fragrant. They mean that the faith in Christ that saves us is the faith of the heart. You cannot any more than this woman answer all the questions about the nature of Christ and his mystic union with the Father; but you can, like her, see the Divine glory in his word and in his works by following Him in the regeneration, and to that faith comes all the knowledge of his nature that is living and saving.

It is a distinguishing excellence of Christianity that it presents to the believer a personal object around which his affections cling. It is not a philosophy of God, but God manifest in the flesh. It is not a dry code of rules and morals, but morality turned into breathing life. How wonderful and how thrilling the thought! that the Infinite Reason should become the word made flesh; should come down into our human conditions; wrap around it the garments of our humanity, and consent to receive our human sympathies and our personal loves. Hence it is that Christian faith is so unlike all other faith, expelling the savageness from human nature, and melting the ice out of the heart, because it draws into itself all the tenderness of personal devotion. Mr. Burke has said, "Nothing is harder than the heart of a metaphysician." So you find it when you compare Saul of Tarsus with Paul to the Gentiles — the first harder than adamant, the last tender as a woman. And yet his creed had not very much changed, but a personal Saviour crossed his path and melted all the flint out of him, and filled his heart till it brimmed over with the love of Christ. And so this humble woman who knew nothing about what they call the hypostatic union, when she saw this Divine Person walking through Palestine took the costliest thing she had and ran to bathe him with its fragrance.

It was heart-faith; and the Master said, "Well done."

But it lies upon us to bring out another aspect of the Christian doctrine. "She hath done what she could." Very consoling words, if we can be sure they apply to us. Very pungent condemnation if they apply not, and we suffer opportunities to go by. The rule demands no impossibilities; but it does demand that every sphere, however humble, shall be filled with divine endeavors. You have not done what you could if you have not made it the problem of every day; how many burdens can I make lighter? how much heart sunshine can I shed about me? how much can I increase the sum of human blessing in the circle where my lines have fallen? How easily we slide into the delusion that we should do a great deal more good if we had the means, overlooking the means that lie close about us!

There is one expression in the words of Jesus in the immediate context which is burdened with a meaning not apparent on the surface. "Let her alone," He says to the meddling disciple with his paltry arithmetic, "she hath wrought a good work upon me." She hath prepared me for burial. As if He had said, I feel better prepared for the agony and death before me for what this woman has done. I am going to the tomb balmed with the love of this humble disciple. "She hath wrought a good work upon *me.*" How wonderful, and yet how very natural! The Christ stood alone; not one of his disciples understood Him. It appals us, almost, to think of the isolation of that awful solitude. And yet this majestic Son of God receives the consolations of human sympathy, and goes to the cross soothed and sustained by the balm of the heart represented by the perfume which this Mary pours over his hair. Most touchingly it betokens to us how much dependence there is on human sympathies where we least expect it and never look for it, and how much the humblest individual, following the promptings of a full heart and on the watch for occasions, may diffuse consolation and light up the circle where God has placed him with the sunshine of the soul. We should cease to be dazzled with the pomps and grandeurs of earth, or think that opportunities only come with great occasions, if by doing what we could we discovered the vast resources of good that lie about us, more precious when found and opened than mines of gold and silver. For observe — it is not generally great benefits and great favors that men need from each other to make their burdens light and sweeten their daily toil. It is the cheering Godspeed, the word fitly spoken, the counsel inspired by brotherly kindness, the wisdom of experience supplied to some one who is losing his way; it is the alabaster box of ointment, that makes the family, the neighborhood, the whole sphere in which God has made us to move, to be filled with the odors of the Gospel. There is more suffering in this world, ten thousand times over, from heart-wants, than from the wants of the body, and there is not a person who hears me who could not do something for another with the box of odors which the largess of an emperor could never accomplish. For there is a great deal of misery which is locked in and treasured up in one's own keeping as something which cannot be helped, but which the precious ointment of humane and gentle sympathies would wonderfully assuage, and perhaps entirely cure. If so great a Being as the Son of God was soothed and helped on his way to the cross by this fragrant anointing, do you think there can be any one who wears this humanity which He wrapt about him, who could not be helped in the same way, in those hours, and they are many, when "the weary weight of all this unintelligible world" hangs hard and heavy upon him? You have done what you could, only when you have been watchful for occasions, and so prevented the gratings of evil fortune over the hearts that beat all about you, by diffusing over them the oil of kindness.

So we bring forth the truth which has its beautiful setting in this evangelic narrative. Briefly we apply it in two ways: —

We apply it to those who waste their time in vain anxieties, morbid regrets, and disappointments at failure. Perhaps there are few earnest minds who do not find out ere the evening gathers about them that life has turned out very different from its early and brilliant promise.

> "I have lost the dream of Doing,
> And the other dream of Done;
> The first spring in the pursuing,
> The first pride in the Begun,
> First recoil of incompletion in the face of what is won."

But so it always must be. The same chasm between the promise and the fulfillment is in the highest heavens; for not the angel nearest unto God has made his deed perfect and brought down all his brighest visions into practice. They have done what they could must be the condition of justification for evermore. Not the things done, but the endeavor, must number us with his angels, for this makes the heavens themselves to be sweet and clean.

But the sermon applies in another direction, to those who have powers they never try to use, beset with occasions they will not see, or seeing, will not turn to account, and to whom come the rebuke and condemnation: "Take the talent from him and give it to him that hath ten; for to him that hath shall be given, and he shall have abundance, but from him that hath not shall be taken away even that which he hath."

IDEALS.

O BRIGHT Ideals! how ye shine,
   Aloft in realms of air!
Ye pour your streams of light divine
   Above our low despair.

I've climbed and climbed these weary years
   To come your glories nigh;
I'm tired of climbing, and in tears
   Here on the earth I lie.

As a weak child all vainly tries
   To pluck the evening star,
So vain have been my life-long cries
   To reach up where ye are.

Shine on, shine on through earth's dark night,
   Nor let your glories pale!
Some stronger soul may win the height
   Where weaker ones must fail.

And this one thought of hope and trust
   Comes with its soothing balm,
As here I lay my brow in dust,
   And breathe my lowly psalm, —

That not for heights of victory won,
   But those I tried to gain,

Will come my gracious Lord's "Well done,"
And sweet effacing rain.

Then on your awful heights of blue,
Shine on, forever shine ; —
I come! I'll climb, I'll fly to you,
For endless years are mine.

XIII.

NO MORE SEA.

REVELATION xxi. 2. *And there was no more sea.*

THE figures of speech which we find in the Apocalypse are not mere flourishes of rhetoric. Regard them in connection with the wonderful experience of the writer, and we find that they symbolize the highest truths of Christianity. We must avoid the error of supposing Divine Inspiration something arbitrary and mechanical, and having no reference to the writer's previous state of mind. John had been the companion of Jesus through his entire ministry, public and private. He drank in his discourses and reproduced them when the eleven could not understand them, and sometimes, where the synoptics only report him partially, or blindly, and in fragmentary portions, John reports with a fullness and intelligence that give soul to them, and bind them together as an organic whole.[1] The figures of speech which glow in our Saviour's language as the types of heavenly things, were preserved in the memory of John and remained there as a living treasure, while the other disciples seem never to have taken

[1] Compare for instance, Mark vi. 32-56, with John vi.

in their full meaning. So when the visions of the Apocalypse were opened to him, these same figures were unrolled before him as an objective world of realities. What Jesus described, John saw, not in written language, but in long perspectives of imagery that made a world in itself. For example, Jesus called Himself "bread from heaven," and "a fountain of water welling up unto everlasting life." Eat me and drink me was his invitation,— language which seemed to the disciples who stuck fast in the letter, mere incoherent speech; and they turned away from it. John treasured it up; and so when the same figures of speech appeared in vision, he saw the tree of life hung with ambrosial fruits to feed the nations, and the river clear as crystal, "coming out of the throne of God and of the Lamb;" and he heard over again the voice of invitation, "Ho, every one that thirsteth come ye to the waters!"

In the text and the immediate connection, if I mistake not, we have another instance drawn from the personal experience of the Apostle. He is on a small desolate island off the coast of Asia Minor,— the island of Patmos. It was a ledge of rocks not much inhabited, the resort since, and perhaps then, of pirates and robbers. Hither he is banished by Domitian, the Roman emperor, and here the vision of the Apocalypse unrolls its panorama. There is a cave shown at this day which, as the monks will have it, was occupied by the Apostle, — a tradition quite as credible, and rather more so than most of their legends. All around him is the sea knocking against this rocky prison with its tumbling waves. Look which way he will there is the tumultuous sea; sea on all sides, not wafting sweet messages, nor the wealth of commerce, but the booty of bandits and thieves. Sleep comes with the thunder of the sea for its lullaby, and he wakes at the music of its roar. The seven churches of Asia are over the sea, with Jesus Christ in the midst of them; the seven golden candlesticks which take their light and trick their beams from Him. The sea, the everlasting sea, is between him and all that is dear to him on the earth. But "I was in spirit," he says, "on the Lord's day," and the higher world of realities broke on his vision. The sea rolled back its waves, away out of sight and out of hearing, and in place thereof he is in the midst of the Paradise of God — and then there was no more sea.

The dreary distances that lie between the Christian believer and the objects of his dearest hope and expectation are most aptly represented in all this symbolization. It brings this subject home to us, — the power of Christianity in turning our earthly Patmos into Paradise. This imagery drawn from the sea abounds through the whole Bible. The old Jewish legend of the Red Sea crossing on the way of the Hebrews to the promised land, only puts into figure and parable our human experience in the journey of life, with the pillar of cloud or the pillar of flame to lead us on. The benefit of this symbolization is, that it interprets to our clearer consciousness much that else were mystical and beyond our comprehension. This surging sea that lies between us and the final rest and fruition, and how its waves are to be stilled, or how it shall cease to separate us from the Paradise of God, shall help us to-day in our interpretations. It represents primarily the unrest within us; it represents the prospect of the future as it appears to our weaker faith, and it represents our insulation and loneliness here on the earth as our friends, one after another, cross over the waves, or seemingly sink in them and disappear. And it provokes the inquiry, how in the highest Christian experience there shall be no more sea.

I. The heart itself, in all its passions and emotions, is a troubled sea that cannot rest until quiet from God comes down upon the waters. There is a stormy ocean that lies between us and Him, and there is no crossing over it while its waves are up. Hence, his first command when He comes to us is a "Peace, be still." What a touching significance there is in that miracle on the lake of Galilee which the painters have tried to render — Christ stilling the waves! The waves are breaking over the vessel and the winds are howling; the disciples are terrified while Jesus sleeps through the whole, and they wake

Him with the cry "Lord save us or we perish!" And He rises and looks over the ranges of mountain billows and looks them down into calm. The Lord asleep in the ship and the ship tossing no whither! So it is in our faithless piloting on the great voyage of life, till we call Him up and He breaks through our drowsy religious consciousness and his "Peace, be still," goes out over the tumbling billows. What a rebuke to the impatience and hurry and reckless plunge through affairs, and the overweening trust in our own cunning or godless scheming with which the business of this world is carried on so largely, while the laws of Providence are lost sight of, and the Christ is asleep in the ship, and panic has seized the crew, and destruction threatens the whole! And how impressively comes the lesson that just in the degree that our turbulence and our convulsive strivings have ceased, the Lord can work in us and for us, and make a smooth pathway for us over the waves. Prayer that really brings God near to us has the least in it of impatience and importunity. It is laying the command of silence on all our turbulence; it is bringing the profoundest hush through the whole world within; and then the Divine footsteps are drawing near, and a Divine form comes walking upon the sea. Peter, foolish and impulsive man, was in a hurry to meet Christ, and in his nervous haste he began to sink. There is prayer so noisy and impetuous, so full of nervous fear, that it never finds God, but on the other hand sinks us deeper and deeper in the bathos of our doubts and passions, as if our noise and our waves of passion and unrest might drown his voice, or surge between us and keep Him out of sight. And there is prayer which is too earnest even for words, when we sink into the most perfect stillness and there is no more tossing of the deep.

> "Not for Him our violence,
> Storming at the gates of sense;
> His the primal language, his
> The eternal silences."

I am persuaded that we besiege the throne too much with our words, instead of trying to find God in the silence that is "golden." We incur the "damnation" of making long prayers. The first condition of finding the peace of God is a profound listening, after all our personal wishes have become speechless. I do not refer to mere musing and meditation, which are very apt to sink into lazy repose. I mean that highest communion with God which comes when our selfhood has been distinguished and rebuked into silence, and our unselfish being through which the Lord speaks, if He speaks at all, our moral sense, our aspirations for heavenly purity, for help in serving others, is all the more urgent, and receives the inarticulate breathings of the Spirit. It is shocking irreverence to interrupt God in his speech; but this we are doing all the while we are piling up our words towards heaven. I wish in all our congregations there was a place for the silent prayer, and I do not know of a more discouraging feature of our social worship, or our conference and prayer-meeting, than our impatience of the still intervals, during which somebody, professedly unprepared, hastens to thump our ears with nonsense. What we need supremely in our daily ongoings, is not some new and more stirring recreation, but a pause somewhere, total and profound, where the quiet from God can reach us as He walks in the cool of the day. Sometimes, when your words are too poor for your thought and emotion, the heart may reach up and lay hold of the Divine promises and the Divine imagery of which the Bible is full; and in that form the soul may be borne upward and lie still at the foot of the throne. It is we that make trouble by too much noise and commotion, stirring the sea within, that casts up mire and dirt from the bottom.

II. But not alone our ceaseless unrest is here imaged forth to us. The mystery of the endless Beyond is here also. Did you never, when a child, stand on the ocean shore, and look off and wonder and speculate as Columbus did, as to what lay beyond that expanse of tumbling and flashing waves? Viewed from the point of mere naturalism, this earth we live on shrinks to a little Patmos of rocks and caves, girded round by a great sea of mystery.

And the imagination conjures up forms grotesque and frightful — just as Homer did when he sent Ulysses into that boundless unknown to find the giants and the monsters, and the hyperborean cavern that opens down into the shadows of hell, and among the pale spectres of departed heroes. Or where there is no imagination to give wing to thought, the vast Beyond is a total blank, the region of emptiness and of — nothing. How mysterious is this sea, with the everlasting moan of its waves, and the wrecks which it holds in its unfathomable deeps! and yet, beyond its horizon, beyond the blue line where the waves seem to touch the sky, the generations have disappeared; our friends and kindred disappear every day, and we gaze after them into the boundless mystery. And what is to push back this line of mystery till it vanishes altogether? Why, there are two faculties slumbering in our human nature, which, being touched by the finger of the Lord, change the whole scene till the line of mystery recedes and there is no more sea. One is the faculty of vision, and the other is the faculty of faith; and sometimes one merges in the other. The beloved disciple had both. His faith was the highest and clearest of the twelve, and so it opened into vision; and what his Lord described in figure and metaphor, he saw where the figure and metaphor became the living landscapes of the heavenly world. And then the rocky Patmos is an island no more. There is a new heaven with its own earth, its own mountains and rivers of water. And who are those that walk beside them, in white robes, reflecting the sunshine of God? "These are they who come out of great tribulation — who have washed their robes and made them white in the blood of the Lamb. They shall hunger no more, neither thirst any more, neither shall the sun light on them nor any heat, for He that dwelleth in the midst of the throne shall feed them and lead them to living fountains of water and wipe away all tears from their eyes." The coast line has disappeared. This faculty of vision was not peculiar to the Apostle. I suppose it to be latent in every immortal soul, and here and there it has been touched by God's finger, and opened, as Jesus touched the eyes of the blind man and made him see. There were such men all through the Old Testament times, and the New Testament times. There were such men among the Greeks and among the Oriental nations. And there was One who had the gift without measure, — without any mists or clouds on his horizon; for Jesus was "in heaven" and on the earth at the same time, — so that He might bring down to earth, and describe to men what He saw amid the eternal serenities, where his higher mind had its dwelling-place. Therefore He says, "We speak what we know, and testify what we have seen." Instead of this faculty of vision, He touches in us the faculty of faith, because vision would blind and dazzle us. When we do not prevent Him by our cries and our turbulence, faith rises clear and comprehending, for it has reason, and revelation, and intuition, and aspiration, all on its side; yes, and the whole line of prophecy running through thousands of years. If you demand certainty, I think it is quite as attainable in spiritual things as in natural. We follow the inductive method. We reason from the seen to the unseen; from facts carefully ascertained, to the conclusions that come from them. I believe Mr. Proctor in much that he tells me about the sun of our firmament and those larger suns that are farther off, and which only appear to me as twinkling stars. I have never looked through his telescope, but I have faith in him as a careful observer, and in the methods of the spectrum analysis which reveal to us the material which other worlds are composed of. But the authority on which rests our faith in worlds that transcend the senses, I hold to be just as unimpeachable, and in addition to that authority we have our own inward beholdings, and the aspirations of universal humanity. Beside the disclosures from above from those whose vision reaches beyond the shadows of time, and whose authority for what they see is as good as Mr. Proctor's for what he sees, are the instinctive perceptions of our progressive being everywhere, and the prophesyings which rise out of it.

They are disturbances and attractions which show a spirit-world in proximity with this, ere that world itself breaks into our field of view. I submit to you, then, that the faiths of religion have the same authentication as the faiths of science, with confirmations that science has not; because the fundamental facts of religion take in those of natural science, and include others which are beyond its range. The coast line of mystery moves off, and our little Patmos enlarges till it touches the borders of Paradise, or crosses over them.

III. But there is a loneliness and solitude that come from this surrounding sea of mystery. Say what we will, we live here on an island, which, as our days increase, shuts us in to ourselves. This whole visible universe is fluid and fluctuating; a "sea of matter" in which endless forms rise and dissolve and disappear. The past generations are the dust we tread on to-day; and the dust we tread on to-day, is to clothe new generations who will build upon our ashes. One half of the northern continents, so the scientists assure us, was an ice floe some hundred thousand years since, which buried extinct races of men whence no tidings have come to us, and the awful cycle is moving round again. I cannot repress a feeling of desolation in contemplation of these inter-glacial generations who know nothing of each other; or of the buried races of humanity, once warm with the fevered life that courses through our veins, but whose dust now makes up the soil we tread and the trees and flowers that grow out of it. How small is the island we occupy in the great ocean of universal being! The whole field of authentic history is comparatively a very narrow space, girt round by an interminable sea which swallows up the generations in an oblivion no earthly knowledge can disturb.

And with the generation to which we ourselves belong, the sphere of our kindred ties and personal relations keeps narrowing in till we stand on one of the solitary peaks, a lone rock in the ocean, with the hungry sea all around it. We start in life young and joyous, clasping hands with a great company; we move on together and the company grows less and less; our hands are unclasped one after another; they on the other shore are more than they upon this, and the solitude grows deeper and deeper till there is one man who stands alone with all his generation gone. How solitary the condition of the old man we read of lately, who had passed his hundred and thirtieth year and sat sighing day after day, because he feared Death had forgotten him and left him companionless in the wide world! The insulation narrows down even to a single spot that juts up in the great sea of being. And why do our friends disappear from us till we stand alone? Because, among other reasons, God can never speak to us in a great company as he can when he finds us in solitude. Did you never, when you had an important message to a friend, call him aside, take him out of the crowd and whisper it low in his ear? Precisely so it is that the Lord deals with us when He comes with his weightiest and most confidential message. There are things which He tells us in the crowds where sympathizing hearts beat in concert, and a multitude of voices blend in one. There are other and deeper things which He tells us when He isolates us, draws us up into his confidence, and whispers to us what no mortal must overhear. There was one man who trod the earth supremely alone,— alone in the crowds, alone in the desert, and alone on the mountains,— for what depths of space lay between Jesus and all the people about Him! And yet through the doors of his solitude what company came! the Father in sweetest and tenderest fellowship, troops of angels, the spirits of just men made perfect. But He did not stay on those heights and in that blest society. He descended from them and brought among the crowds and into all the activities of the world, the spirit which came from the baptism of solitude, and followed him like a halo along his path. And that is the way He deals with us. The more complete my isolation, the more profound should be my listening, assured that the Divine lips are close to my ears with a message. And this is just the way the great and the good who have attained the most have left behind the superficial culture, and the mere echoes back and forth which come from the crowds, and ascended the heights of an individual faith on which the peace of God rests forever. Though not the vision of Patmos, yet the faith which carries its divine scenery in the soul and makes us strong for duty and abolishes death, is there. The narrow bounds of our little island recede away, and away, till at death they disappear altogether, and then — there is no more sea.

The sea of *unrest*, the sea of *mystery*, and the sea of *separation*, are to disappear in the Apocalypse of God. But let me not speak without qualification and reserve. Unrest and mystery and separation there must always be, though I trust all that embitters them here may be left behind. There is the unrest of the soul which is always athirst for higher things, for enlarging and more sufficing knowledge, and for deeper draughts of the River of Life. It is the unrest that keeps us from moral indolence and the sleep of spiritual death. It is the earnest of all our higher attainment, but without the fever of our consuming cares. There is the line of an ever-receding mystery as the domain of knowledge enlarges. As the day gains upon the twilight, the twilight shoots faint rays into the total darkness and makes a new twilight to be explored. But total darkness there must always be except to Him who inhabits eternity and fills infinity with his presence. But the mystery will no longer torment the soul with the cruel doubt and despair that becloud the face of God, and shut out his paradise from view. Faith will never be lost in sight; for however high the heaven we attain, there will be a yet higher one for faith to apprehend and for the soul to reach after. The sea of mystery will only recede and lie on a remoter horizon. Insulation there must always be, for there can be no meeting and recognition of the friends who have gone before into whose society our individualism shall be altogether merged, or which shall keep us from those serene and solitary heights where God meets us betimes alone and takes us up into his eternal refuge. Unless we are to go up to these mountain peaks and drink there the purer ethers, society, though of the angels themselves, would cease to be a mutual excitement to higher things. We must dwell sometimes apart or we cannot dwell with others, though it be in heaven itself, with that giving and receiving which insure to society a progressive life and joy.

The voice of the celestial multitudes, then, could it fall down upon us and become audible, would come in words of cheer. It would tell us that the Divine dispensations are the same for earth and heaven. The strengthening angel from among them would be the angel of Patience, and his message would be, "We have not only passed through the same that you have, but we are passing still. Unrest and Mystery and Insulation are with us as with you. They are the Divine ministries by which you are to come up hither, and by which, after you have joined us here, we are still to journey on forever. Be guided and purified by these ministries as we have been ; be with us in spirit even now, and then for the unrest in its corroding anxieties, for the mystery that imprisons within the coast-line of storm and darkness, and for the insulation of loneliness and desertion — THERE IS NO MORE SEA."

PARTED.

A. M. M.

How dread the silence! — on the shore
    We stand and shout in vain!
The voice that cheered us once, no more
    Will answer back again.

If sainted ones their memories keep,
    And love's most sacred vow,
Why yawns the gulf so wide and deep
    That parts them from us now?

Methinks the silence speaks, " My share
    Of griefs and conflicts o'er,
Why should the waves of mortal care
    Break on the heavenly shore?

" In all the works that I have done,
    My spirit pleads with thee;
Go finish what my hand begun,
    Then come and reign with me.

" Another Hand with touch divine,
    Knocks softly at thy door;
A voice of deeper tone than mine
    Pleads with thee evermore.

" And in its sure prophetic tone
    It tells of things to be,
When to the heart bereft and lone,
    There shall be no more sea."

NOT LOST BUT RISEN.

M. L. P.

"We would not call thee back"—so let them say,—
   What the lips speak the bleeding heart denies;
My voice, dear friend, should call thee back to-day,
   Could it but reach thy dwelling in the skies.

For we have need of thee: thy radiant smile
   Lay like a sunbeam on this scene of care,
And weary burdens at thy touch erewhile
   Were changed to burdens light as summer air.

Thy pupils need thee: for thy careful hand
   Removed the thorns and scattered fragrant flowers,
And their young minds beneath thy clear command
   Woke into conscious life their noblest powers.

Thou needest us, dear friend: through pathways bright
   Far, far away from us thy feet have roved;
But thy new friends among the sons of Light
   Can never love thee more than we have loved.

Soul to its place, dust to its kindred dust!
   Such is the law and we will not complain,
But ever clear of Time's corroding rust,
   Thy love we cherish till we meet again.

For through the parting veil we see thee now,
   In thy fair clime, with faith's unclouded eye,

See thee with every "charm of mind and brow
   Baptized anew in immortality."

And thou art risen, another, yet the same,
   Nor have we lost thee in thy heavenly birth;
The woman there who takes an angel's name
   Is still the friend that we have loved on earth.

XIV.

THE CHRISTIAN CHURCH AS A MEANS OF PROGRESS.

MATTHEW xvi. 18. *On this rock will I build my church, and the gates of hell shall not prevail against it.*

THIS text, perhaps, has been the occasion of more persistent controversy than any other passage in the New Testament; and vast systems of church government are supposed to be based on its authority; and yet, when we clear the text of some obscurity, partly through false rendering, the meaning seems exceedingly simple and plain. The original word here rendered "hell" is not the one which describes the retribution after death. It is "hades," which means the realm of departed spirits generally, without any reference to their condition. Rendered into modern language we should read, — the gates of the spirit-world. This, in language which drops the figure entirely, is simply death; for death is the gate, or entrance, to the spirit-world. Our Saviour's declaration, then, is simply and clearly this, My Church shall be built on such foundations, that it shall never die out. It shall continue from age to age, and never fail from the midst of men.

How wonderfully have these words been fulfilled! States and empires, and human institutions of all kinds, have risen and fallen, while the Church remains; and though its enemies have kept predicting its downfall, or its waning and vanishing life, it has lived on with cumulative power, sometimes making a conquest of these enemies themselves, and drawing them over to its side; and its increase and influence were never greater or more pervasive than to-day. Its form, its methods, and its temper have changed, and will continue to change. Its foundation and its innermost essence and substance are ever the same.

For what *is* the foundation, the " Rock," on which the Church of Christ is built, so strong that the waves of time beat against it in vain? A very few words of exposition will serve to show. In one of those hours of clearer and higher enlightenment among his disciples, Jesus asks what the people are saying about Him, and how they themselves regard Him. The people, say his disciples, rank Him among the prophets. " But whom say *ye* that I am?" Peter, whose name literally rendered is Rock, replies at once, " Thou art the Christ, the Son of the living God." On this confession of the Christ, Jesus replies, " Thou art Rock indeed, and on such a rock, that is, such a confession of me, I will build my Church, and so constituted it will never die out." That is to say, — such acknowledgment of the Christ will be the foundation of the Church in all ages. He is such a want of all humanity as the ground of faith in spiritual things, that this confession of Him will continue to the end of time. The Church so founded — this is the meaning — shall be such a necessity in the world's affairs, shall have such adaptation to the deeper wants of the soul, that it shall never decay.

In unfolding this subject, we will first lay off and leave behind us some false or partial conceptions about the Church, and then come to the essential Church idea, and show why it lives on forever, as one of the necessary means of human progress.

The idea which some people have of it seems to be, that its main object is to celebrate the death of a Jewish prophet and reformer who suffered martyrdom eighteen hundred years ago. This, with a profession of discipleship, constitutes a church. By and by, however, the question occurs, Why should we keep celebrating the death of one martyr, or one prophet, especially one who lived so long ago, when many since have taught and died for their race, — men of illustrious virtue and sublime self-sacrifice? No valid or sufficient reason can be given. And so in some congregations the Church idea fades out almost entirely, and its rites become meaningless. Unbelievers make their assaults upon it; but always you will observe their blows are directed against this empty shadow, while they have never even caught sight of the substance itself.

Again, there are diverse forms and methods, each claiming to belong to the true Church, and to be essential thereto. Who is to decide which is right? The question is often asked, as if the essential Church of Christ were a lo, here! or a lo, there! as if any fixed form were indispensable, and not rather the spirit and substance whose form can change according to the life within, in adaptation to the wants of the age or the condition of men. Moreover, all that is said about the corruption of the Church pertains not to the essential Church idea itself, but to human weakness and depravity as obstacles in the way of its complete realization.

I. Coming to the heart of our subject, we say, first, that the essential idea of a Church is that of a Divine Person, around which it may be gathered and organized. Abstract ideas may organize a school of philosophy. A Church requires a supreme and living Head. And a Christian Church has for its Head the living Christ; not a dead Christ who was buried centuries ago, but who is the Mediator to-day; in whom the soul has access to the Infinite Father, and a personal and conscious experience of his abounding love. It is the Christ risen and glorified, and therefore nearer the mind and heart of the believer than he ever could be in the flesh. Again and again Jesus avows such inexistence of the Father and the Son, that to lose the Son is to lose the Father, while to know the Son is to know God with a knowledge so intimate that it is like seeing Him openly. And this mediation of Christ was not limited within the thirty-three years of his sojourn in the flesh. Rather his incarnation was the preparation for a mediation more complete in behalf of all humanity till the end of time. "Lo! I am with you alway, even to the end of the world." "It is expedient for you that I go away, for if I go not away the Comforter will not come." He means evidently, that from the risen and glorified state, the Holy Spirit was to come through his mediation as never before. The Christ, on the spiritual side, was to be so marvelously nigh, as to bring the disciple into relations with Him, and through Him with the Father, more intimate and tender than they had ever conceived. "I in them, and thou in me, that they may be made perfect in one, that the world may believe that thou hast sent me."

If any one supposes that this language is that of metaphor, and as such is to be explained away, he has only to turn the pages of subsequent history to learn his mistake, and to find a full commentary upon the Saviour's words. It is a fact of church history more conspicuous than any other, that the presence and mediation of Christ, and fellowship with Him was altogether more plenary and sunbright after his ascension than before; that men who had never seen Him in the flesh, felt his power to mould their natures anew, and give them a profound consciousness of the pardoning mercy. "But that was a great while ago, and before the first enthusiasm had begun to wane." He who says this knows little of the course of Christian history; of the deeper and deeper channels it makes for itself, and is making to-day. Not by open vision, like that of Paul and John, but by the deepest and warmest intuitions of believing souls, this same consciousness of the mediating Christ in the midst of his Church gives it power and conquest now, and is fulfilling the Saviour's prediction, "Lo! I am with you alway." Those who say the most about the shortcomings and corruptions of the Church, and with too much truth, do not seem to be aware that they are urging a most weighty argument in behalf of its living Head, and the duty of gathering in nearer and more trustful relations around Him. The corruption, the errors, the cruelties of men! what thick and baleful clouds has He melted through, and melted away, and cleared off from his path, as He comes down through the ages! The sins and wrongs and misconceptions which gathered before Him, measure somewhat the aggressive power of his truth and grace, in making a way through them for the New Jerusalem to descend and be the tabernacle of God with men. All this He foresaw in the long perspective, and foretold. False and persecuting religions were to take his name, and profane his truth, only to be cleared off by its power as his own church descended and prevailed, enrobed with heavenly charities and beloved as a bride. The thickness and the blackness of the clouds that gather about the rising sun, and put bars in his way, illustrate his power in breaking through them, and finally clearing them out of sight in the warm glories of the noontide.

God in his infinite essence can be approached by no finite being. He cannot come to us by moving his own substance into us, for that would abolish our own personality. He comes to us by forthgoings out of his own essential being, and this gives us life and salvation through the medium which makes tender adaptations to our condition. Nature is such mediation; the angel world is yet another. But the one perfect and all-sufficing is a Perfected Humanity, through which the full supply stands over against every want of the human heart, and through which the Father reveals Himself in those human qualities which He could transcribe into our finite natures to bring us into correspondency and communion with

Himself. In declaiming against the Divine Personality, there are some who forget that if man in his most perfect state is in the image of God, God must be in the image of man, and that they are trying to divest Him of every attribute of Divine Fatherhood, till faith has been emptied of all its contents and become a vanishing shade. Christ is "the image of the invisible God," "the first-born of the whole creation," in whom dwelleth "the fullness of the Godhead bodily." And as such He is the central Life around which his Church is gathered and organized, and through whom the Divine Love flows forever.

II. Given a Divine Person around whom we can be organized in the bonds of discipleship, and in whose mediation our communion with God is full and free, the idea of *fellowship* can have its complete realization,—that interior fellowship of heart with heart and mind with mind which makes the ties of brotherhood something more than a theory and a name. It is that brotherhood of souls in which the weakness of each is supplied by the strength of all, in which our individual one-sidedness is complemented by the all-sidedness of the whole, in which the wants of the heart are supplied by a common and abounding love. There is the good-fellowship of the world which knows men only as social beings, as inhabitants of the earth in the enjoyment of its pleasures and friendships; church fellowship involves the idea of human beings as immortal and spiritual, with deeper wants and yearnings, and capacities for higher pleasures and satisfactions than the world knows of, and deeper need than it can supply. The Church of Christ, therefore, truly such, is a home for the soul where kindred souls are to be met, and where the great Friend of all souls abides in spirit, flows into all hearts and draws them together. Here it is that all artificial distinctions are prostrate, and every heart can open to every other heart for counsel and guidance. Here it is that the hunger of the soul for human and Divine love has had its richest supplies and satisfactions; here it is that the weary burdens of this world have been made light in a common sympathy; here it is that its temptations have been disarmed; and here it is that the soul has found the opening gateway of death not a lonely and dreary passage, but has entered it amid loving farewells. If you doubt it, read the interior history of the Christian Church, — not its ecclesiastical annals, — and you will find that the Christian communions have been the illumined summits where heaven and earth have met together, and the promise, "Lo, I am with you alway," has had its continuous fulfillment. Music and song here touch the deeper chords of sympathy, — those which chime with the songs of victory before the throne, that almost become audible, and render the Church on earth and the Church in heaven but one communion.

III. All this being given, the Church aggressive

and militant, and arrayed against the evils and unbeliefs of the world, is sure to appear. The disciple of Christ does not seek a home-centre of the heart for selfish ease and repose, nor for the mere luxury of fellowship. He is there invigorated and furnished for the work of conquest, not only over the evil in himself, but over the evil in society. Fighting in our own name and with our own weapons, we become swollen with conceit and self-assertion, or we relapse into cowardice. When you have the whole brotherhood behind you, and the Christ in the midst of them all and inspiring them all, your personality is as nothing, but the spirit that breathes through the whole supplies your weakness and bears you along with it. What would you be, or what could you do in the business of life, if you had not a home to go back to betimes and to start from anew? And how much more elastic your step, and how much surer your aim, when you know that the sympathies and thoughts of kindred go with you, and are ready always to give you a welcome home! But the Christian Church in the supreme sense is the home of the soul; for there the brotherhood of souls is organized in the name of Christ, and there He comes with the inheritance of his Spirit to keep the way ever open between earth and heaven. Home is the basis of all our best activities; and this is just as true in the higher sense of the great Christian family as it is in the lower and narrower sense of our private families and affairs. It is a place to go from as well as a place of retreat when wearied with work. You come back to it that the heart and the mind may be replenished for new forthgoings and conquests. There is no missionary spirit unless there is a Church to kindle its fires and keep them bright and burning. All the great reforms originate in the Church, and go from it directly or indirectly. Even those reformers who have repudiated the Church and denounced her for her short-comings, would be only empty declaimers did they not draw from the armory of Divine truth which the Church preserves and transmits to the ages. For if you lose the doctrine of a Divine Fatherhood and the doctrine of human brotherhood in Christ, who claims every child of God, not for this world alone, but for an endless life, reform sinks into measures of mere temporal expediency; it is a mere plea for creature comforts, or the battle-cry of political parties, and has not the sanctions of the Eternal Justice. What are the rights of man as a sharer only of the good of this world compared with those which inhere in his nature as an heir of immortality? That the Church has failed sometimes to apply faithfully the great truths committed to her keeping, that she has failed even to understand them in all their just relations, is only saying that her members are finite and human; that there is One in the midst of her greater than she is, drawing her up nearer and nearer towards the heavenly ideals, and prophesying through endless time to guide the nations to their goal. And by a law as sure as the law of gravitation, illustrated by the facts of history, when men get away from the Christian Church and the records and treasures of truth of which she is the guardian, and which she brings down through the centuries, they lose any such clear and vital conception of God and humanity and the relations between them, and the relation of man to an endless future, as clothes him in angelic dignity, or makes him anything more than a higher developed animal to perish with the brute natures of which he is kith and kin. The grand truths which make man worth dying for, which make the sacrifice on Calvary, and the martyrdoms on all the high places of the earth no waste of blood, but sweet and beautiful offerings for human salvation,— these truths, if not lost, get exceedingly blurred and out of sight except as the Christian Church guards them, preaches them, applies them, and transmits them to after ages as the inheritance from a Divine Mediator.

IV. "The gates of hell shall not prevail against it;" that is to say, it will never die out of the world. It is eighteen hundred years since these words were spoken, and I want now to glance one moment at the signs of their fulfillment to-day. I see it stated on careful authority, that the ratio of increase among the churches who acknowledge most fully the divinity and mediatorial nature of Christ is far in advance of the increase of population ; while religious bodies which have not this foundation, have no such increase, but either dwindle or fade out of existence. Their ratio of increase falls vastly behind that of the population, and points to their final extinction in the progress of society. This is a fact of the highest significance, and it disposes at once of all the declamation we hear about "the advanced ideas" that are to supersede the organized Christianity of to-day. The organized Christianity grows strong and pervasive where the living Christ is its central power and influence; where He is left out, the fires flicker and die. But there is another fact still more auspicious. Mere increase of numbers is not always a sign of real progress. Increase of spiritual power certainly is; the life that inspires the charities and humanities that overrun the lines of sect, and make all the denominations only the divisions of one army of the living God, waging battle, not against each other, but against sin and unbelief, and all that hinders the complete coming of Christ into the world to redeem and save it. These are signs of progress, and they never shone brighter than now. The kingdom of Christ is not merely aggressive without — it comes within. It is melting out the sectarian hardness and exclusiveness that keep Christians apart, and is drawing them together in one great catholicity. It is the New Jerusalem descending from God out of heaven these eighteen hundred years, and now touching the earth as never before.

It is not the conquest of one denomination over the rest, but Christ coming among all through an interior way, and bringing our partial theologies into more genial conformity with his own absolute Christianity. These are the real tokens of progress within and without, and they fill the earth with the signs of a redeemed and advancing humanity. Not that any denomination has reached the absolute truth as it is in the mind of its Author. But it is characteristic of the New Era, that the denominations start from their agreements, not their divisions; from Christ as the luminous centre, and thereby come into the currents of that new fellowship of the Spirit which takes the old hardness out of them and clothes them in the comprehending charities of the Gospel.

Such are the signs of the continuous fulfillment of the prophetic words, "The gates of death will not prevail against it." I wish they could have a continuous fulfillment now and here. If you would make this church an organized and increasing power in this community, you, my Christian friends, brothers and sisters, must do something more than sit still and look on from the outside. You must come into it; breathe your souls into its fellowship, and assume your responsibilities as Christian disciples. The Christian Church, however, can do without you; you cannot do well without it. I doubt if without it Christianity can be a completely transforming power in your own hearts and homes. A confession of Christ I believe to be a prime condition of a full reception of Him ; for our beliefs, which are only abstract and speculative, become indistinct and vanishing ; they are living and operative when we put them into our life before the world. " Whosoever," He says, " shall confess me before men, him will I also confess before my Father which is in heaven ; but whosoever shall deny me before men, him will I also deny before my Father which is in heaven." What a profound truth we have here verified in the history and experience of to-day! To confess Christ heartily and practically is to come into a living and blissful apprehension of the Divine Fatherhood. To deny the Christ is to have the Divine Fatherhood obscured, and even the whole Divine Personality lost, or merged in the dumb forces of Nature. The word Father stands no longer for a conscious Divine Intelligence, and then the heavens over us are black as night, and man is an orphan. A confession of Christ brings you not only into new personal relations with the Father, but into such new relations with the whole Christian brotherhood in earth and heaven that the Divine life which throbs through it shall be yours also. For in this matter of Divine and Christian fellowship, we must give if we would receive ; and if we will not give any, we must freeze in our isolation. He that saves his life loses it ; he that gives it out freely, makes it abound even to the life eternal.

SONG FOR THE COMING CRISIS.
(1858.)

O Church of Christ, to prayer, to prayer! lean on thy sacred shrine,
And there while lowly bowing down, receive the strength divine:
Then rise and let thy faithful word be healing for our woes,
And let the Spirit's flaming sword be lightning on thy foes!

Hark! in the horologue of Time, God strikes the awful hour!
Zion must now stand face to face with Moloch's threat'ning power;
The subtle snare of compromise her hand and tongue that bound,
Breaks clean away, and now her feet take hold on solid ground.

And there she stands — aye, on the Rock where stood God's Church of old,
When seas of blood dashed at her feet, and waves of trouble rolled,
There let her speak in that great name which faithless men profane,
And they who scoff at Freedom's Word shall wag their tongue in vain.

By the blest throngs of pilgrim ghosts that haunt New
England's air;
By pilgrim graves o'er all her hills and down her valleys
fair;
By all the pilgrim's faith in God that burns within our
souls;
By every drop of pilgrim blood that through her bosom
rolls,

No hunters here for human prey to snuff their trail of
blood;
No laws to grind the helpless poor and break the laws of
God;
No tyrant's troops to line our streets or tramp our valleys
green,
While Bunker's shaft looks from the sky down on the
shameful scene!

Ring with thy bells a swift alarm from every crashing
spire,
And speak with lips which God's right hand has touched
with coals of fire;
Let Christ's whole Gospel be proclaimed, let God's whole
truth be shown,
And let the East and West respond and echo tone for
tone.

Then rise, O Church of Christ, arise! shake off thy slumbers
now,
God's conquering strength within thy heart, his calmness
on thy brow;
In Christ's dear name who died for man, put all thy glories
on;
No bondsman's blood upon thy robes, no stain upon thy
lawn!

HYMN.

(FOR THE ANNIVERSARY AT PLYMOUTH IN 1853.)

BENEATH the hallowed ground where now ye tread,
  New England's first and holiest martyrs sleep,
And ocean waves to celebrate the dead
  Lift the eternal anthems of the deep.

And here their mighty spirits linger long,
  They walk abroad through all the hallowed air,
And where a pulse for Freedom beats more strong,
  Know ye that pilgrim blood is coursing there.

O ye whose sacred dust on Burial Hill
  Kind mother Earth in holy trust contains!
Above the cause ye loved keep watching still,
  And roll your fire through all our languid veins.

Then from New England's hills, afar and near,
  A light shall stream in columns to the skies,
And like a new Aurora, shall appear
  Where'er a race in chains and darkness lies.

XV.

IDEALS OF WOMANHOOD.

JOHN ii. 4. *Jesus saith unto her, Woman, what have I to do with thee ? mine hour is not yet come.*

THIS whole scene is abundantly significant and suggestive. This and one other are the only instances in the New Testament where we get any glimpse of the character and person of Mary the mother of Jesus. John records here the displeasure of Jesus at her officious intermeddling with Him in his work. The rebuke which his language certainly involves was strong or mild, all depending upon the tone and manner of its utterance. It is not implied in the word "woman," for that was a title of honor and dignity; and our Saviour uses the same word in that most tender scene at the cross, where He commits his mother to the care of John, " Woman, behold thy son ! " The words of rebuke in the text, rendered into the plainest English, would be, " Woman, do not interfere with me in my work." But the words might have been uttered, and doubtless were, in such tones of respect as to exclude all harshness, or lack of filial regard. The narrative implies that a good deal more was said; that this was not the first instance of interference, and that John has been very reticent, and thrown a veil over the weakness of Mary.

You observe in all the narratives how Jesus designedly avoids calling her his mother. He never addresses her by that title. In another instance of similar interference, while Jesus was in the midst of one of his sublime utterances, his mother sent in word that she desired an interview with Him. The message seems to have interrupted his discourse. "Thy mother and thy brethren stand without, desiring to speak with thee." But he answered, "Who *is* my mother and who *are* my brethren?" And then, pointing to his disciples, "Behold my mother and my brethren;" as if saying, I acknowledge no relations but spiritual ones, no bonds but those of humanity. And again, after one of those discourses which thrilled the multitude by its power, a voice broke from the crowd, "Blessed is she that bore thee, and the breasts which nourished thee;" when Jesus put in a sort of disclaimer, "Rather blessed are they that hear the word of God and keep it."

From all this we infer that Mary had the weaknesses that belong to human nature; that some of them were so prominent that they needed reproof and palliation; that Jesus treats her with tender regard, not merely because he was born of her, but because she was a woman, brought into special personal relations with Him, and a partaker of the common humanity He came to redeem. I suppose that by thus ignoring the maternal relation, He simply claims that all his endowments are from a Divine Fatherhood. As if He would say, "All that I am comes from the paternal side. No matter how weak, or how low down the humanity which I have assumed, I owe nothing to it but the clothing through which the Divine Word is embodied and revealed." The nature and character of Mary have no more to do with the life and character of Jesus than those of any other woman. We do not know that she was exceptionably good, though she might have been, notwithstanding her weakness. The Eternal Word, descending into this world to redeem it, must needs be born into it; but it received no education from human fathers or mothers, and no taint and mixture of our depravity. And so Jesus calls Himself "the Son of God," "the only begotten Son of God," but never the Son of Mary. By virtue of his human birth, He calls himself "the Son of man," — a generic title, importing that He inherits not the nature of one man, but of humanity in the complex, that He might become conscious of the whole range of wants, sufferings, and temptations, which through Him were to be supplied with strength from the fullness of the Godhead.

The ideals of a true and perfect womanhood, what they are and whence they should be sought, is a subject suggested by the text, and one of exceeding interest. If once we can put away from us the ideals which are false and illusive, and bring fairly before us those which are true and inspiring, we shall do much to solve one of the problems of the day. Let us enlarge for a few moments on each of these two topics. First the false ideals and then the true ones.

I. Perhaps four fifths of the Christian Church relapsed early into Mariolatry, and they remain in that worship still. Not the Roman Church only, but the Greek, and portions of the Protestant, draw hence their ideals of perfect womanhood. The reasons of this are very obvious. The office of Christ as a Mediator had been made so official and technical and exclusively theological as to take Him out of the sphere of our humanity, or any genial relations with it. So the want was still felt of a Mediator ; one of tenderness and gentleness and humane sympathies ; such as do not belong to our coarser manhood, but which are the very essence and inspiration of the highest and truest womanhood. And Mary comes in to supply the place ; not any Mary that ever lived, but one who embodied the highest conception which the Church then had of the perfect woman. And it is vain to say that the influence of this idolatry was altogether bad. In times of cruelty and theologic hate, what a persuasive must it have been to tolerance and mercy! When the priesthood was corrupt, and when men like Charlemagne, who were held as the models of virtue, had the stains of blood on their garments, there was at least one form of human nature which was held aloft and worshipped, and which breathed of gentleness and charity. Not any Mary that ever lived, but an ideal womanhood, gathering into itself some of the holiest feminine attributes, Mercy and Charity and humane sympathies, was enthroned among the idols of a corrupt and sensuous age; and when the attributes of God and of Christ were both lost sight of, and the means of knowing them from the Scriptures were in the keeping of a corrupt priesthood, that sweet and beautiful ideal of womanhood shed its lustre among the cruelties of dungeons, scaffolds, and battle-fields, and did something to soften and to mitigate. It hung on the walls of churches; it melted through the imaginations of cruel and sensuous men as a heavenly vision pleading for humanity.

On the other hand, how defective and one-sided are these ideals, and how liable to abuse and degradation, inspiring the devotion of cloisters and nunneries, and a dried up virtue that wants healthful blood and out-door freshness! The saints after this model became intensely conscious of their piety and sanctity, wore halos around their heads, with a rolling up of the eyes, as if they were too good for the earth, and did not really belong to it. No inspiration comes hence, infusing energy for the great conflicts of life and strength under its burdens.

In one of the most celebrated art galleries, after passing one picture after another of saints in attitudes, with halos about them, holy families, and Madonnas in robes of artificial sanctity, you come at length to one of the grand historic scenes, setting forth the old Roman idea of womanly virtue. It is the death of Virginia. On the other side is Junius Brutus passing the death-sentence on his two sons for treason; all suggesting how clearly and sublimely the old stoical virtue could rise above the weakness of kindred ties and the bribes of self-interest. Its ideals were not the highest, but our weak, sentimental Christianity has hardly improved upon them. I think they come in as a mighty relief after those other models of cloister piety and devotion kept and nourished for shrines and postures.

II. But false ideals all aside, we come to the question, Where shall we find the models of that womanhood most worthy of our admiration? Christ was a pattern of the perfect man; where, if not in the mother of Christ, shall we find the pattern of the perfect woman? Shall we look along the ages and take the Virginias, the Rebeccas, the Marys, and the Joans, put them all together in order to make out the ideal which we are in quest of, very much as the sculptor takes a grace here and a contour there from the best patterns he can find? The very question suggests how deceptive are all models and all outside patterns, and that the standard towards which we aspire is to be sought in some other way. Christ, it is true, is the perfect man, the full-orbed humanity. But even He does not present Himself to us as a model. He never asks us to imitate Him. Imitation of other people's virtue is nothing but a kind of mimicry after all, and never opens in the heart the original springs of piety and goodness. "If any man thirst," says Jesus, "let him come unto me and drink; for he that believeth on me, out of his heart shall flow rivers of living water." Inspiration, not imitation, is the privilege of the hearty Christian believer; and inspiration unfolds all the best possibilities of our nature whether of men or women; unfolds each on its own line of organic growth and development. It does not make women into men, nor men into women; but it makes men more manly and women more womanly, drawing each into those excellencies and perfections for which the hand of the Creator originally attuned their natures. Neither men nor women are called to do just the things that Christ did, and do them in just the way He did; and if we attempted this our mimicry would appear fantastic enough. But Jesus as Mediator draws us up into full intercourse and communion with the Divine Nature itself, in which are all the perfections of both halves of our finite humanity. Avoid the absurdity of making Christ one God and the Father another God;

but regard Christ as the manifestation of the whole Divine Nature, all its energy, all its sweetness, and all its tenderness; the Fountain of all that is good in father or mother, or brother or sister, or man or woman or child, and then the worship of God through Christ brings forth the graces of each one's nature that belong to that nature and none other. The vine and the oak which it clasps and adorns both drink the same sunbeams; one does not become the other by growth and culture, but each grows into its own kind of perfection and grace. Woman is capable of a kind of perfection that men never can reach; of diviner sympathies especially as they embrace infancy or childhood, divining its wants and woes and all the fit ministrations to human suffering. Men are capable of a kind of perfection that women are not; I will not say a lower kind, but more outer and tangible, and which pertains more to the understanding than the heart. Women reach conclusions through intuition and perception, men through logic and induction — a slower and more circuitous way. And even in the discharge of the same duties, each sex has its own style of doing things, and when one undertakes the style of the other they cease to act themselves. The evil of all man worship or woman worship is to make the worshippers one-sided and untrue to themselves, and if they attain morbidly in one direction they are sure to become lean and shrunken somewhere else. The ideals which we ought therefore to follow are those which dawn continually upon our rising faith as they are let down to us every day out of heaven. They are on some line of action to which you will be sure to be called as a follower of Christ; called by the spirit of Christ within you, and the standard of duty which shines on before you. They are not patterns which you get from outside; they are the angels of God's presence that beckon from above and call, "This is the way, walk ye in it." Perhaps it is a way which nobody ever walked before with the same step, because ability and opportunity have not been given to others as to you.

All the disputes about the equality of the sexes come from the conceit which some have that manly excellence is of a higher order than womanly; that the head is nobler than the heart; that intellect is a higher attribute than love; that muscular power ranks higher than moral power; that the mind which plans for brilliant campaigns and great military achievements, or for building roads and bridges, and making money and subduing physical nature, ranks higher than the spirit of goodness, without which all power is only brute force, and the highest intellection only contrivance for pomp and show. It is bad enough for men to claim this supremacy; it is worse when woman is seized with the same ambition and tries to grasp it, instead of accepting the royalty which God and nature have given her, which wears the highest crown, and which rules by diviner and less vulgar methods. God is love; and love is his highest attribute, because it inspires and gives direction to all the other attributes. It is this which is given supremely to woman, and she descends to a lower position whenever she renounces its prerogatives.

What is it to be a follower of Christ, then? It is to be brought in Him and through Him into a more full communion with God, so that out of the Divine Nature our own natures are supplied and impleted, and all their heavenly possibilities are unfolded. Men gain strength and energy to be men. Women gain strength and energy to be women. Matrons become better mothers when they put on Christ, because the parental instinct is then purged of selfishness and gains wisdom and direction. Maidens rise to a purer and nobler maidenhood when they put on Christ, because then they forget themselves in a Christian calling that gives scope to all the womanly graces and virtues, and they are saved from the vanities of worldly show. The Mary Wares and Carpenters, or the Marys of any age, do not follow their Christian calling because some outside pattern has been held before them, but because through the Christ they had a profounder baptism into the Divine love, and were inspired to do the promptings which it gave them. What the Church needs now and ever is inspiration; the soul of goodness put into its enterprises, its charities, its schools, its worship, its missions, its forthgoings to save the world and redeem it ; and woman is doubly responsible for this, because her nature is, or should be, more receptive of the Divine goodness, and ought to make channels for it through all the ways of the world.

There is a very beautiful custom observed in Catholic countries, of keeping the churches open on week days, so that people can come in and kneel and worship at any hour, and go away strengthened and refreshed for their duties. Opposite the great York Minster is a Catholic church, famous as the one in which Guy Fawks was baptized. Beside the high altar is a statue of Christ, in the features of which are more of benignity and Divine Majesty than I ever saw put into marble. It was very touching to see the market women from the street, one of them halt and lame, totter along the aisles, and come and kneel before it, and then go away with brightened features to their humble work. In a remote corner of the church was a shrine to the Virgin, and there went the delicate ladies to kneel and mutter for the hour, not imbibing strength for the burdens of the day, but to get a draught of sentimentalism for an indolent devotion. And this, I think, represents two kinds of worship, one bearing up the soul through a full-orbed and perfect humanity to the Father of all, the other exhaling in raptures before ideals which have the strength and majesty taken out and our finite weakness put in their place. One ends in mere sentiment; the other goes with us where we take up our burdens, and makes them light and easy.

As to the ideals needed most for the womanhood of our times, and the work of to-day, I think there is no room for mistake. Men become coarse, earthly, and cruel, where women are frivolous, selfish, and worldly. Men become brave, just, and honorable, where women shed abroad the grace, the charity, and the self-sacrificing spirit of the Gospel. Family affections become enlarged and ennobled into philanthropy with maternal and sisterly tenderness breathed into them, where Christian womanhood presides in the household. Childhood takes the impress of heaven and grows into the bright image of God, if unfolded beneath the moral power and moulding of a Christian womanhood. It is apt to take on the coarseness of masculine vices and depravities, where mothers renounce their charge to a lower order of minds that *they* may have time for pleasure and amusement. Compassion towards all that suffer, whether man or animal, or bird or insect; intolerance of any needless pang in any creature that breathes, — these are full and operative where woman's nature has its rightful baptism in the Divine Love, and this compassion fails from its channels, just in the degree that woman fails from the duties of her sphere. Higher than any sphere which modern discovery can open to her, is this inmost and highest one whose shrine has no fit priesthood when she fails from it, and through which come the unction and the inspiration in all the lower departments of human activity. The freedom which woman should demand is to do and to be all that Christianity in its full reception inspires her to do and to be ; for then she will demand nothing which is unwomanly or which is not congenerous with her nature in its pure and heavenly development. No danger then that she will cease to be herself, or that she will fail to fulfill the demands of her whole being. The work of moulding the faculties, when young and tender, of evoking the powers of childhood, whether in families or schools, is preëminently hers ; and it is a higher work, because a more interior one than that which is done in legislatures or on battle-fields ; for without it the legislatures and the battle-fields would be lacking in the virtue and the consecration which save them from becoming the scenes for the wrangles and strifes of older children. " Behold my mother and my brethren," is still the benediction of the Master upon those who are doing the Father's will, each according to the methods of his original genius, enlarged and sanctified by the Christ within. Men have lectured and legislated upon intemperance, one of the crying evils of the day, and from which women suffer more than men, because their sensibilities are susceptible of deeper and more cruel wounds. We have long felt that this reform needed a soul to it, a moral suasion which could find deeper springs of action and melt through the sordid selfishness of men with diviner touches. Do not say that woman may not supply the very element we need because of the irregularities which thus far have attended the new methods of reform. There are always irregularities where the deepest inspiration and the loudest cry of God through the soul must beat against the iron bars of a brute conservatism, and break through them to get free. What real men ought to say to these women is, as it seems to me, "Godspeed you in your work! May you succeed where we have failed! We will do our best to prepare the way for you, that the voice of the Spirit may have its utterance and sweep this evil from the land!"

Ideals of womanhood! They come down from heaven every day and every hour; they grow brighter and warmer as your Christian consciousness grows clearer. Follow them as the angels of God's presence, no matter into what new and original fields of beneficence they beckon you; no matter what barriers must be broken through, if the voice of the Christ in you is calling you to work with Him and gain the victory! Do you say that the world will laugh, or that public opinion bars you from your appropriate sphere? But what is the laugh of the world but the "crackling of thorns under a pot?" And as for public opinion, it is what in large measure you make yourselves, and would to God you had made it better! More than any man or all the men together, you make the fashions of the time, and you make them run to show, and the lavishment of expense on the flaring vanities of earth, and take away just so much from the higher culture, and from the means of making light the weary burdens of life. There are reforms yet to be achieved, which require no renunciation of Christian womanhood, but demand that it be put on in its completeness and beauty, as you follow Christ in the regeneration.

GIRLHOOD AND WOMANHOOD.

I.

WHAT strange magic brings before me that old school-
house on the green,
While the dusk of time is gathering over all that lies between?

Seats adorned with rustic carvings, shaky clapboards old
and gray,
Smoky walls and broken windows and the pig-weeds by the
way,

Little griefs of little children felt beneath the tyrant's
rule,
Or the big boys', who were hazers of the ancient country
school.

All the squalor and the sorrow of that earliest fairy-land,
Change within the magic sunshine; all the dirt is golden
sand.

What were pedagogues and hazers! faces bright were al-
ways there,
And the morning came new risen from the face of Ellen
Clare ;

She the tall and beaming maiden, whom we always ran to
meet,
Just escaping from our cradles on our little twinkling feet.

They may sing of gentle ladies holding court at castle
    hall,
But our country-girl was peerless, and more gentle than
    they all :

For she brought the bloom of orchards in the glow upon
    her cheek,
And we thought of golden robins every time we heard
    her speak ;

As she smoothed the tear-wrought channels where our
    sorrow had its flow,
And brought sunshine o'er the faces which the imps had
    scoured with snow.

Dancing-schools, and dancing-masters ! — pastures with the
    lambs at play,
Or the breezy heights and ridges, where we climbed the
    summer's day.

Singing-schools ! — among the orchards, with the birds at
    matin-time,
Or the morning stars together singing to their march sub-
    lime.

So she danced with breezy motion, breezy as the light ga-
    zelle's,
And her singing soared the sweetest over all the village
    belles.

O, the memories of our childhood coming thick and mani-
    fold,
Drifting westward down the valleys fleecy clouds that turn
    to gold !

II.

They wandered east, they wandered west,
  On prairie, shore, and sea;
One sleeps beneath the ocean's breast,
And some have found the last long rest
  Beneath the willow-tree.

Beside yon hill that cuts the air
  With its blue curving line,
There lives a maid; she once was fair, —
She's fairer now; her silver hair
  Has caught the heavenly shine.

Her song of cheer still rises clear,
  In hymns of softer strain;
Where sorrow sheds the bitter tear,
Or where the spoiler's step draws near
  The couch of mortal pain.

Where anguish needs the cooling palm,
  Or worn and fevered care;
Where sin pines sore for mercy's balm
There will you find, through storm and calm,
  The paths of Ellen Clare;

With heart to weep with him that weeps,
  And love with him that loves: —
Why one deep chord its silence keeps
Ask not of me; ask him who sleeps
  In ocean's coral groves.

O'er Ellen's cot, on yonder height
  The evening star stands still,

And flames in larger lustre bright,
Before it looks a last good-night
And drops behind the hill.

Even so thy life, O lady blest,
 Pours its last beauteous ray;
Its evening glories are its best,
As sinking to thy heavenly rest.
They melt from earth away.

XVI.

THE DIVINE LIFE-PLAN.

ROMANS viii. 28–30. *All things work together for good, to them that love God, to them who are the called according to his purpose. For whom He did foreknow, He also did predestinate: . . . . whom He did predestinate, them He also called: and whom He called, them He also justified: and whom He justified, them He also glorified.*

IF a peasant, on some clear evening, were to look up to the heavens, he would see nothing but a wilderness of lights, — stars and star-dust, strown at random through the fields of space. The main work of science is to detect in this wilderness the principle of arrangement. And as far as this is done, every drop of star-dust becomes part of a system, and there is no atom that is not in its place, and doing its work in the universe. Just so it is with events; with all that enters into human history and experience. Our human life seems at first chaotic, and things happen to us according to no principle of order. But all our later experience goes to detect this order, and could we see the whole, no event would stand separate, and all the star-dust would be formed into worlds.

It is not much to have a mere general acknowledgment of a Divine Providence. There is no Christian doctrine more abused and perverted, for there is hardly any calamity which flows from human wickedness which is not laid off upon the Providence of God. We are very apt to lose one grand and vital distinction. There are two kinds of Providence, acting according to the free-will and purpose of man. There is the Providence which leads on, marks out the way, urges, compels even, by shutting us off from one line of action, and shutting us in to another. Then there is the Providence which only follows; which allows a thing to be done, but does not lead on to its doing; which will not break in upon man's agency, though he plunge into the blackest crime, but goes after and mitigates. Hence, there is a directing Providence, and a preventive Providence. One leads us if we will be led. The other follows us whether we will be led or not, keeps its hand upon us, and subordinates even our crimes to its eternal purpose. You will observe in the text, it is the Providence that leads and draws us on which is described; not that which would prevent merely, but which would attract and win; not Calvin's dogma of decrees, but God's adaptations to man, by arranging the events of life according to his supreme and heavenly order.

I. A divine plan is distinctly marked out, within

which every regenerating man is drawn and kept by a chain that cannot break. Mark the steps. " Whom He did foreknow, He also did predestinate: whom He did predestinate, them He also called : whom He called, them He also justified : and whom He justified, them He also glorified " Let us pause a little upon these terms. They have been petrified into dogmas. But rightly rendered, they give us a Christian view of life so much above the times of the Apostle as to avouch its Divine origin ; and we shall alike admire its sublimity, and be soothed with its consolations.

" FOREKNOWLEDGE." With God there cannot be any foreknowledge which comes from forecalculating future events ; for God, unlike us, sees events wrapped up in their causes. If an acorn could be transparent, and you should hold it up to the solar microscope, you would see in the germ of it the future oak outlined distinctly in all its branches. And in a handful of acorns you would see perspectively the lofty and wide-spreading forest. So, doubtless, God sees all that is to be ; the whole future in the present ; things to be are as things that are ; all that we are — beneath the deepest scope of our self-consciousness, is open to Him, and therefore He knows all that is to come of it. For our natural life, down to the smallest events and happenings, is but the flower and foliage of our spiritual life, even to the branches and the stems and the fluttering leaves.

" PREDESTINATE." More rigidly rendered, limited

beforehand. And the meaning is, most clearly, the Lord prearranged our life-plan, so that all events should be fitted into it, and every thread and fibre in a man's surroundings be so woven and adjusted as best to secure the end. This is the preordering, exactly suited to the most propitious unfolding of one's spiritual being.

"CALLING." This is more than arranging events for us and adjusting circumstances. It is God speaking to the inward mind, now open to the tidings of higher things. It is the Divine law lying audibly upon the conscience. It is that stage of the human experience sure to come with every man when there is the call and the answer between God and his child. On one side, "Hearken to my voice!" On the other, "Lord, what wilt thou have me to do?" The solemn period this, when you wake up to the necessity of moral choosing by that voice within the soul which comes louder than the sound of many waters over the clamor of our self-interests and passions.

"JUSTIFIED." Better rendered, made righteous; for that comes when the calling is obeyed; not an imputed and make-believe righteousness, but being made an obedient subject of the law of Right, laid with supreme authority upon the conscience, making you yielding and pliant under it as a little child.

"GLORIFIED." This, in Scripture-phrase, has a meaning exceedingly definite. It is not translation into some heaven of material splendor. What it means we know very well from what is called "the glorification" of our Saviour. That was when the inmost Divine Life came out in all its fullness, in place of the lower and earthly life which it displaced forever; and then He was transfigured to his disciples, or to John, in vision clothed in heavenly majesty. So of his followers. To be glorified is to have our highest, most heavenly frames, pass over into the outward life and practice, till they become the Christian's daily habit, his spontaneous adornment, and grace. "Be ye transformed," says the Apostle, "by the renewing of your mind." It is the outward man transfigured by the inward, taking the colorings of the spirit within, and the clothings of its light and beauty. It is when our moralities are not mere duties and tasks laid upon us, but the outgoings of the heart and reflections of its love-light alone. Before we reach this we do good and talk good outwardly and by compulsion of law. Now the Christian changes into the image and likeness of his Saviour, even as the shining ones. Before this, in the figure of old Cudworth, we are like dead instruments of music, to be played upon by the musician's hand. After this, it is as if "the spirit of music embodied itself in the instrument and lived in the strings, and made them of their own accord dance up and down and warble out their harmonies." And observe how being glorified follows after being justified; how the all-beautiful law is first laid upon us outwardly to be obeyed as a command, but afterwards enters inwardly as our life and love. In the words of Job, "I put on righteousness and it clothed me, and justice was my robe and diadem."

These, then, are steps on the stairs to heaven. Such is the Divine plan that involves us. And you see how one stage follows on the one before, and grows out of it ; how the Divine knowledge that sees all our future in what we are, weaves about us the life-plan adapted to its end ; how that brings us to the place where his voice becomes audible, and He calls ; how obedience to the call brings us obsequious under the all-plastic law ; how this, from an outward rule, becomes an inward and renewing life, till our daily moralities reflect its light, and are glorified in it. Such is the perfect plan into which God seeks to put each one of us ; into which He does draw every soul pliant enough for the mouldings of his Providence. And I think you will agree with me that the consciousness of being involved in such a plan as this gives an indescribable dignity to human life, and makes its meanest adjuncts, down even to the dust and the straw we tread on, to glitter with a light which is not their own ; that the house which is the humblest and whose furniture is the meanest, if only its work come into this plan and arrangement, borrows a lustre from above, and must seem to God's angels who look down upon it as when the sunlight blazes from cottage windows. There is no waste page, no stray leaf from your book of life. You must see, if involved in such a plan, how it lights up all your cares, hallows all your griefs, dignifies your most servile labors; for it takes them all up and unifies them in a system that works for immortal ends. As quaint old Herbert says, —

> "Who sweeps a room, if this the end,
> Makes that and the action fine."

When Columbus was on his first voyage of discovery and was approaching the shores of the New World, he was steering straight towards the Florida coast; but at that time a flock of sea-birds flew across the track of his vessel. "Methinks," said one of his men, "that here is a sign from heaven. Something tells me we ought to follow the track of these birds." Columbus partook of the same superstition and turned his keel. In so doing he turned in some sort the destiny of two continents. He turned the whole course of modern history. And if in shaping the future of a continent down the long centuries in its customs, laws, and language, there is a Providence that guides the sea-birds in their flight, will you not believe that in our personal history, as He leads us and ripens us for heaven, not a sparrow falls on the ground without your Father?

We come, then, to a truth of exceeding interest. Men are ready enough to acknowledge in the gross that God has some system of the universe and takes care of it. Why will you not see the particulars which this general truth involves? If this be so, why will you not see that He has a special plan for each one of you and tries to keep you in it? Every man by his original make and capacity is unlike every other man, and needs therefore a training and development of his own; needs some adjustment of circumstances unlike every other man; so that the good which is to be wrought out from his condition, and the character to be formed from it, shall have original shapings and colorings. To be saved in the full meaning of that word is not merely to get to heaven, but to have wrought out the special end and to have formed in you the individual excellence which God made you for. He has not only his plan of the universe, but his plan of each man's life, and from behind the veilings of his Providence is leading him in ways that he does not know; giving him temptations, trials, crosses, joys, and sorrows, which are all his own. The thought may startle us at first, but the inference is inevitable from our subject, that He not only marked out the pathway of the worlds, but that your path and mine were sketched in the Book of God before we entered them.

II. But we are not like the things of nature held passively in the Divine plan. We can take ourselves out of it if we will. That is to say, we can renounce the Providence that leads us, and place ourselves in that which is only sequacious and preventive. One, as I said leads us and urges us. The other follows us. One draws, incloses, organizes our whole life, physical, spiritual, and eternal, into its own supreme order. But we can renounce all this. We can break away from God's order and try to make one of our own. We can renounce his plan and follow our own self-will. Shall not his Providence still fold us in? Yes, but it is no longer the Providence that goes before and draws us; it is that which goes behind and looks after us. The first entices us with all heavenly attractions. The other follows on after evil, tempers it, balances it, subordinates it, and keeps it from a lower abyss. The field of the one slopes upward into the heavens; the field of the other slopes downward into the deeps. In the one, man is an end in himself, and the Divine purpose is wrought out within him. In the other, this end has so far failed, and man — as in the case of Pharaoh — is degraded into a means and instrument of something else. In the one, the Divine Providence confers the greatest possible good; in the other, it prevents the greatest possible ill. The directing Providence draws him who tries to climb upward, engirds him with invisible helps, makes his foot firm on every stair where he plants it, till he stands on the serene summits at last. The preventive Providence still places an arm under every man that falls; breaks his fall, and lets him down the abyss with the least of wounding and laceration, for there is no malignity in the punishments of God. So the Psalmist, "If I ascend into heaven, thou art there. If I descend and make my bed in hell, behold thou art there."

I hope the distinction is plain, but I illustrate. Some years ago a vessel went to the South Sea Islands with a Methodist missionary who felt impelled by a Divine urgency. He carried the good news of Christ to a people who lived by murder and ate human flesh. By incredible perseverance and sacrifice, he gained many of them, and they were changed into Christian men and women. There was another vessel that sailed to the Guinea coast where the crew landed to burn negro villages and capture slaves, and they opened the slave-trade which has been kept open till now. I suppose you will agree that the Divine Providence did draw the good James Calvert into his work and worked with him, and was a guard of fire about him in his perils and sufferings till the curses of cruel men were changed to sweet and tender songs. And you will agree, I think, that the Divine Providence did not urge John Hawkins to his work of man-stealing, yet followed him in the bloody track and blackened wastes which he left, to bring all possible good out of ill; to temper evil; to subordinate crime; and to make the tophet of slavery work at last in the redemption of a race.

Such is the twofold Providence. On one side the view opens upward to the foot of the throne; on the other downward out of sight. Its golden links involve us if we will yield to them, and then they are sure to draw us upward to the blest abodes.

If my subject has come home to you, it has prompted a very practical inquiry. Where in this twofold Providence am I included and involved ; in the one which directs and draws me on, or that which only follows and mitigates ? that which pulls us up the heavenly stairs, or that which only lets us down the easiest way through the lapses of sin ? These questions can be easily answered, and let me go on now and seek the tests by which we can answer them candidly and fairly to ourselves.

1. If we are indeed in the foldings of the Providence that directs and urges, we shall be very likely to invoke it, study its signs and manifestations, and be on the watch for its leadings. I do not mean that it will break into our life-plan openly, for then it would overwhelm us with its splendors. But no man who looks up daily with the prayer, " Lord, what wilt thou have me to do ? " is left very long without an answer. How very different it is with godless and worldly men ; how they keep plunging on and on, with no other guidance than their own self-will ; and hence so much of the hurry and fever and scramble in the race of life. Hence the alternate elations of success, or depressions of disappointment, or anxieties and bodings of disaster, by those who never allow those pauses in their affairs, when in the

hush of the hour the Divine voice could be heard, and the Divine tokens could be clearly seen. It is said that, as a people, none are subject to so many accidents and surprises as we. If it be so, it is because we have less of this hush and listening for the Divine leadings, but have blotted out the word Providence and written "luck" in the place of it, and so the door is left wide open for all the devils of confusion to come in. It is a most instructive fact, that the men around whom events seem to marshal themselves and conspire together to one end, are men who have been in the habit of looking for and following a Divine lead, till finally it comes to them almost consciously, transfused through their very intuitions, and the Divine calm comes down upon them and lies about them, where the confusion and the surprises cannot enter. Indeed, the more we seek these Divine leadings, the more they will draw us up into the Divine counsels, so that under the shadow of that Rock which is higher than we, we can watch the motions of the tides and the dashing of the waves, and feel secure with our finite reason, folded in the Omniscience of God.

2. Again, if we are involved in that Providence which leads and directs, it will shape all our conceptions of the discipline of life. For I suppose all persons come to look upon this world either as mere pleasure-ground, or as a school where immortal beings are educated for the skies. How differently

from these two stand-points will they interpret all the events of their probation! From the one the question always is, How do they affect my enjoyments? From the other the question always will be, How are they affecting my manhood or womanhood, and my attainments for immortality? How different seem our crosses, trials, and failures, from these opposite points of view! From one they are so much dead loss, so much abstracted from our pleasures. From the other they fit in and harmonize in the frame of our history, and make a single mosaic where we love to trace the finger of our God. Regard life as a school and you soon come to ask the meaning of all its environments even where they touch you most painfully. "How did I need this, and what is the message which it brings to me? How does it fit to my inner life, and what is the good I am to extract from it?" Even the great sorrows that come over us like a cloud, will not be black with the wrath of God, but they will rather come with those soft droppings of the rain, under which we are sure the tender blade will shoot forth, and the greenness of another spring.

3. There is another test, and a very definite one. What the Apostle terms the Divine call, comes to every man somewhere in the unfolding plan of his life. Yea, God prearranges and preorders our life-plan, so that this call shall somewhere be very distinct and audible. It is true, no man ever gets quite

out of the hearing of it, though the Divine voice is muffled and obscured in the whirl of our interests and passions. But how, clear as matin-bells, it sounds through the young conscience as yet unspotted from the world! How sharp and pungent are its urgencies where the young man or young woman stands at the parting of the ways! free to choose the whole business and work of this earthly probation; free to make this world a mere field of pleasure or a field of discipline, where all the faculties are trained for humane or divine employments. Here it is that vows of obedience and self-consecration, distinctly taken and recorded in the Book of life, put you in the Divine plan; so sure to draw you up the heavenly stairs, that the old theologies name it by such words as "effectual calling," "irresistible grace," and "Divine decrees." Indeed, they very well might; for think what ministries watch over you and wait round you when once such a vow has been decisively made and recorded on high. Then the Providence that leads and draws is ever with you, for all the happenings of your probation are so toned and organized as to help you on. For as the Apostle puts it, the invisible heavens, then close round you to get the victory for you, and in his list of co-workers he places life, death, angels, principalities, height, depth, things present, and things to come. All these become yours. And how great is the sin and the shame if, when such ministries watch round us and wait to enfold us, we break out from their charmed circle to where no Providence can lead us, but only follow after us ; not to give us his best, but only keep us from our worst in the gulfs of ruin.

These tests are very simple ones. I think they are very decisive, and I have tried to make this distinction in the twofold Providence of God sharp and clear, because we are so apt to slide into the world's cant which is only a pernicious fatalism making "all things for the best." They are for the best when we put ourselves within the grapplings of the golden links by which He draws us. They are the best when we have given up our plan for his. Then how blessed it is to live! for that majestic repose called the "peace of God" will be ours. Our consciousness will grow brighter and more profound, that we are living in God's life-plan, not ours, and that we are drawn into the central calm of the world's confusions where we hear tidings of invisible things, —

> "Of ebb and flow and ever-during power,
> And central peace subsisting at the heart
> Of endless agitation."

ABOVE THE STORMS.

Above the storms and thunder-jars
  That shake the eddying air,
Away beneath the naked stars,
  Rises the Mount of Prayer.

The cumbering bars of mortal life
  Here break and fall away,
And the harsh noise of human strife
  Comes never: Let us pray!

Father, may thy serener light
  Reveal my nature true,
And all its pages, dark and bright,
  Lie open to my view.

I've mingled in the battle-din,
  That shakes the plains below,
And passions born of earth and sin
  Have left their stains, I know.

How silent move thy chariot wheels
  Along our camping ground,
Whose thickly folding smoke conceals
  Thy camp of fire around!

We tremble in the battle's roar,
  Are brave amid its calm;
And when the fearful fight is o'er
  We snatch thy victor-palm.

On surface knowledge we have fed,
    And missed the golden grain ;
And now I come to Thee for bread
    To sate this hunger-pain.

No gift I bring, nor knowledge fine,
    Nor trophies of my own ;
I come to lay my heart in thine,
    O Lamb amid the throne !

All that the Father hath is thine, —
    Thus does thy word declare, —
So the full stream of life divine
    Flows from the Godhead there.

The tree of Life, in mystic rows,
    Stands in eternal green ;
Out from the throne the River flows
    In crystal waves between.

Ambrosial fruits hang o'er the waves
    That pour their cleansing flood ;
Thy Fount of Love the heart that laves,
    And fills with royal good.

That good I seek, yet not alone
    The hungered heart to fill,
But as the angel nigh the throne
    Made swift to do thy will ;

Thy will, unmingled, Lord, with mine,
    That makes all service sweet,
And charged with messages divine,
    Puts wings upon my feet.

No need to trim my taper's blaze,
No need of sun or moon!
The glories falling from thy face
Make my unchanging noon.

XVII.

HOME.

LUKE xv. 20. *And he arose and came to his Father. But when he was a great way off, his Father saw him, and ran and fell on his neck and kissed him.*

THIS portion of Scripture is generally called the *parable* of the Prodigal Son. I very much doubt, however, whether we are to take it as fictitious narrative. We find in the Gospels two kinds of parables. One kind is drawn from the processes of nature, such as Matthew and Mark report — the lilies of the field, the leaven, the wheat and the tares. Another kind is drawn from transcripts of human life, such as the good Samaritan, and the prodigal son, and these might have been both history and parable. They may have been such narratives of fact as had come to our Saviour's knowledge; and this may have given a directness and pungency to his teachings and their application. There seems little doubt that the story of the good Samaritan was a narrative of this kind, and we see at once how straightway it went to the conscience of the priests of the temple who came to listen and cavil. The story of the two sons reads much like history, — one of them very correct and moral, but proud, selfish, and cold-hearted; the other profligate and generous to a fault, but more quickly convinced of his fault and more easily brought into affectionate and child-like obedience. The Jewish and the Gentile believer are here strongly typified, and the story is put home to the Jewish conscience encased in its bigotry and pride.

In the times of our Saviour there was one foreign city where a young Jew would resort to perfect his accomplishments by foreign travel and knowledge of the world. It was Rome, drunk with her abominations, gone down in sensuality, and glaring in false splendor. If our young hero went by way of Greece he probably would have spent his living there already without seeing Rome. There was enough at Corinth of lust and profligacy to absorb his substance. There were swine-herds in the country to give him employment; and it was regarded as the lowest business a man could engage in. Starved, and beggared, and in rags, he finds his way back to Judea — his pride all broken down, and doubtful as to how he will be received. Something like this is the family history, a chapter of which our Saviour has extracted to turn it into parable and hang on it the Divine truths of his religion. They are all there, — every one of the essential truths of Christianity has here its image and setting, and in language ever dear to human affections. Without trying to exhaust the meaning of the parable, or draw out all the doctrines of Christianity which cluster about the narrative, we will attend to one practical lesson which appeals to us with special urgency. It is the power and influence of Home in the moulding of the character, and even the regeneration of the whole spiritual nature. Its direct influence we are ready enough to acknowledge; its indirect, unconscious, all-abiding influence, we are somewhat slower in perceiving. Our young Jewish traveller has forgotten home for a while amid the revelry, we will suppose, of some Grecian city. At Corinth, lust was even enthroned and worshipped, and temples were built and dedicated to sensual pleasure, and in the midst of these debaucheries all the purer and sweeter memories of his childhood are drowned and lost. But his substance gone, and naked and starving among the swine-herds, there is one spot that looms up like a brilliant star away over the sea and over the hills, and calls him to a better life. It was not some exhortation to virtue from a Greek moralist that brought him to repentance; it was not the memory of some sermon he had heard in the synagogue; it was the awakening of home memories, and they came so persuasively that he takes the resolve at once, "I will arise and go to my Father." And what was the magic of these home memories?

There are a great many kinds of homes, but

for the most part they may be ranged in four classes. There are places where people simply inhabit under the same roof for the purpose of eating and drinking and sleeping. They have no other end but to procure for themselves, in the most convenient way, food and raiment and lodging, and that done, the end is secured. Getting a living only means getting enough to eat, drink, wear, and inhabit, and for this purpose there must be some place to lodge nights and keep comfortable. That is one kind of home. There is another kind. There are homes which are places of instruction and discipline; where getting a living is a means to this discipline; where example and precept are both used for the training of children in the way they should go; places of education for the coming responsibilities and business of the world. It may include religious instruction, discipline, and example. Then home becomes a primary school where successive generations are prepared for the duties of life. That is another kind of home. Again, there are homes where the affections of the heart are lavished, where each lives in all the rest, and all live in each; where each finds his own nature complemented and supplied in its lackings and shortcomings, and where the relations of husband and wife, and parent and child, and brother and sister, are lines of communication for mutual help, and for the sunshine of the heart to flash over them.

So there are places to lodge in, places of discipline, places for mutual love; and there is almost always a kind of unity which belongs to every one of those little societies which we call families. The members get moulded, consciously or not, by the general spirit which pervades a household and keeps it together. If it be only to supply the animal wants, if that is the main thing which gives unity to the house, it will be very hard for any member of it to escape the coarseness and the touch of animality affecting the taste, the style of thought, and the style of character. The children will breathe it in, and they cannot help it. People may seek to cover over this coarseness with paint and finery, and pictures and culture; but behind them all there will be the moral squalor that cannot be concealed, and there will be a taint of earthliness in the whole atmosphere of the house, which no ventilation from open doors and windows can ever drive out. Or again, if instruction and discipline and example are supplied, and these are all, and give their tone and spirit to the household, the atmosphere of the house will be cold and chilling, and lack sunshine. Even a good example, when cut to order, has no magnetism in it. A school is a very good place in its way, but a school is not home and is not society.

Or again, if family affections and mutual helps are all that give unity to the house, the family becomes a smaller clan for building each other up, living in each other, but living in nobody else; and so the atmosphere of the house may be heart-warm, but it is the warmth of self-love reflected back and intensified. Indeed, I do not think there is any form of human selfishness that grows into shapes so stupendous, and at the same time so deceptive and imposing, as that which is nourished by these family affections left merely in their natural state, and with no higher inspiration to give them soul, expansion, and guidance. Even the forms of charity and religion may be only the outside decorations of family show, and the sweet offices of domestic love may be only the natural instinct of the heart, blind to everything that transcends the narrow sphere of family interest and pride.

So, then, there is still another kind of home — one which takes up what is good in these three and supplies something more. Put all these three together, — a place to lodge in, a place of discipline, and a place of family affections, and something else. Make it a seminary for immortal beings to be trained and prepared for an endless existence; not only to do business in this world and do it well, but for the highest duties and employments of any world, whether on this side of the River, or on the other side, for it makes no difference. A good life here is the same as a good life anywhere; for to do our work on earth and do it well, is to bring into full employ the powers of mind and heart which are put into the employments of heaven itself. Suppose this conception of home to rule it and give it unity, the mind and character of all in it will be formed in yet higher mouldings. Then there is another Being who will dwell there. Then even the drudgeries of life lose all their coarseness, because their end and purpose are to get the foothold and foundation for the education of immortal minds. Christ will be in it and fill out all its business with his own Spirit of grace and love. Example will not be a pattern of conduct cut to order and exhibited before children for them to look at. Example will be the spontaneous outbreathings of the Spirit of Christ, always the same, whether the children are in hearing or not — even as the rose always gives out its fragrance and beauty, though nobody is passing by. Discipline will lose all its hardness, though none of its firmness, for it will be the loving tractations of a hand guided by gentleness, of a spirit which has the Divine patience breathed into it. The family will not only be a school, but a society where minds and hearts open into each other, in order that each may find what is wanting in himself, and in order that the faults of each may find their rebuking and repression in the atmosphere of truth and affection that pervades the house and fills it.

And family affection loses all its clanship when

the Christ is in it, because the love of kindred enlarges to a love of kind ; yea, the more you love your own household, the more just and loving and forbearing will you be towards other households ; for you will see more keenly and know more perfectly all the tender and sore places where the world chafes against the sensibilities of other people, and how its wrongs affect them in their dearest and tenderest relations. The great reformers and philanthropists have generally been those whose philanthropy has been kindled at home, who have enlarged the ties of kindred into those of kind, and learned in the brotherhood of the family the brotherhood of the race, and how grievous are the sins and woes by which its ties are cankered or wounded. Every new birth in the household now becomes sacred, for every babe that enters it is the fresh bud of immortal being, and baptism assumes all its beauty and significance. Indeed, the baptismal rite is as full of meaning as the funeral rite, for it takes the little being out of the category of mere animal existence, and receives him from the Great Giver as an heir of immortality. When friends go out of the world, we dismiss them with rites recognizing their spiritual nature, putting in our hopes of their hereafter. How fitting, quite as much, that the new-comers into this world should be welcomed with rites which symbolize their spiritual being,— buds to be opened into immortal flower. Maternal love becomes something more than blind instinctive affection, for it is enlightened, guided, and inspired by another love, pure as an angel's, and giving to it an angel's unconquerable strength. Prayer and family devotion become more than a set form and prescribed duty ; for a family so unified, and organized for such an end, becomes a society on earth, brought into alliance and correspondency with the blest societies above ; its life is their life, their spirit is one and their worship is one, and family prayer is the open door through which the invisible messengers come and go, and the Holy Spirit descends. The world itself has recognized the fact that about some families there is an invisible guard which their philosophy has not been able to account for. The home so organized, and for such an end, subordinating all its employments thereto, has a unity of its own. It will have its sorrows, its trials, its bereavements, its chafings and corrosions, but the one spirit and end hallow them all, and turn them to some account in the Divine economy ; and amid all the darkness of this world there will be a light in the house and all around it, as when cottage windows are ablaze to the distant traveller and cheer him on his way.

The influence of a home like this cannot be measured by any visible and palpable results. Its influences are not merely restraining, but regenerating ; for they store up a host of memories and associations which, though buried for years under worldliness and depravity, will wake up afterwards, and sometimes fill the whole soul as with the chime of angel-voices. They are the very things stored up and kept secure, which the Holy Spirit afterwards takes hold of and uses for the conversion and regeneration of the soul. I doubt whether any soul is ever lost whose advent into this world is through a good home. It is seldom that there is any falling away from it; but even if there is, the coming back will be through the language which time may have obscured and covered over, but whose letters blaze out anew when, by trial, by sorrow, or by repentance, the obscuring veil has been withdrawn.

There was another son which history tells us of, who did not go to Corinth, but away down into Egypt, to be surrounded also with seductions to sin, and with the trials of evil fortune. But he resisted the temptations, and turned the trials into moral victories so brilliant that they shine down through all the ages. And whence came the strength that girded him and held him up? Why, there was a home away up in Judea, where not only the love of parents, but the love and fear of the Lord, had been stored up and kept in the most tender places of the heart; and this was what the Lord Himself laid hold of, not only to save the boy, but to save a whole nation from extinguishment.

The family is a Divine Institution, and there is no substitute for it. It is older than any other institution. Every one of you, by Divine appointment, is a member of it. It is older than the State, older than the Church, older than Universities, and the parental line is more sacred than that of any Apostolic Succession, and goes up higher and away beyond it. The Christian duties which pertain to it you cannot delegate to anybody else, and by no ingenuity can you find anything that will supply their place. You cannot *send* the children to Christ, but you may lead them along and draw them after you. The home lies back of the Sunday School, and its teachings run through six days and all the twenty-four hours, and the tide of interest in the school rises and sinks with the life in the homes that inspire it and throb through it. You may give the children books to read ; your own book of life they are reading all the while, perhaps more thoroughly than you are aware of, for their clear innocent gaze will take in the very lines and chapters which you may think are most obscure. The unconscious influences of home, those which come from little things, little speeches, little deeds, and little offices, "that best portion of a good man's life, his little nameless unremembered acts of kindness and of love," are more subtile and pervading and plastic over the character, than the teachings which we set ourselves formally to make. For it is not merely from what we say or what we do, but *how* we say it and *how* we do it, and in what spirit and temper, that the life of our life comes out and shows its quality. You may shape the young lips to prayer, but the young eyes will see whether your life is a prayer and an aspiration towards heavenly things. You may give them hymns to learn, but it will come to nothing if the music is drowned in the discords of earthly passions and the din of this world. We may teach them here the Saviour's "Come unto me;" we work against mighty odds if they see you either going the other way or halting and standing still. And there comes a time, a very solemn time, when the home breaks up and forms anew; not only the cradles are brought in, but the coffins are carried out, and there is to be sorrow and mourning, and heaven is to be seen through tears. And you are to live in this world long after you have left it, — live in the memories you leave behind you, memories which may be a long and sweet persuasive to things which are pure and lovely and of good report; yea, the very chairs where you sat, and the pictures on the walls, and the old blessed Bible that lies on the stand, shall speak long afterward and call others to Christ in more tender accents, if only now you will fill the house where you live with the fragrancy of a Christian life. But for this Christ must come into the house now to be learned there and taught there, and lived there, and He must shape the very end and purpose for which all its business goes on and all its burdens are borne, even to make the home on earth a seminary for the skies.

The subject has a broad and forcible bearing upon every one; for who is there that has not wandered away from the house of the heavenly Father, and wasted the substance He has given; these powers of mind and heart, these means and opportunities being unused or misused, instead of being consecrated to the ends for which He gave them. And are there none of you in that land of want and famine who have yet to put forth decisively the power of choice, in that high resolve, "I will arise and go to my Father?" And are there no voices that call thee back, no remembered tones of a Father's spirit that has been grieved away; no remorse for perverted, or wasted, or slumbering powers; no fading ideals of a purity and innocence that make thee sigh for peace with God and rest in his atonement; no images that throng down from the hills of life's morning land and make thee long to be a child again in thy Father's home? like the man, who, reposing on the field of strife during the truce of battle, went back in his visions to the scene of his early innocence, —

"And knew a sweet strain that the corn-reapers sung."

"FEED MY LAMBS."

Ho! ye that rest beneath the Rock
  On pastures greenly growing,
Or roam at will, Christ's favored flock,
  By waters gently flowing:

Hear ye upon the desert air
  A voice of woe come crying!
While cold upon the barren moor
  Christ's little lambs are dying.

"Go feed my lambs!" — the Shepherd's call
  Comes down from realms of glory.
"Go feed my lambs! and bring them all
  From moor and mountain hoary."

Fast falls the night, the bleak winds blow
  Across the desert dreary!
Great Shepherd! — at thy call we'll go
  And bring the wanderers weary.

GLAD WORSHIP.

O God of Love ! we bless thy word that hallows
    This day of rest to our o'erwearied powers :
As comes thy calm down on the foaming billows,
    Come to our souls thy sweet Sabbatic hours.

Here may the aged ones, their griefs forgetting,
    Breathe in the quiet which thy temple fills ;
And may their sun when near its tranquil setting,
    Clothe in its farewell smile the western hills !

May childhood learn the words by Jesus spoken,
    And give to Him the fresh and morning hours
Ere sin the earliest charm of life has broken,
    And while the dews lie sparkling on the flowers.

And here may all — strong man and blooming maiden,
    When with the load of care or sin opprest,
Hear Jesus' voice, " O come ye heavy laden,
    Come unto me and I will give you rest."

And passing on through Earth's brief joys and trials,
    May these thy people join the immortal throng
Who sweeter incense waft from golden vials,
    And worship thee in their unending song !

I WANT NO FLOWERS.

I want no flowers thy stone to wreathe,
   Nor on thy grave to blow,
And mind me of my withered rose
   That turns to dust below.

I need no picture on my walls,
   Thine image to renew,
And mock thy dear angelic smile,
   And eyes of tender dew.

I want no spectre-form to come
   In glimpses of the moon,
Nor message breathed from lips of air
   That melt and vanish soon.

If these be all that Mercy leaves
   To soothe our great despair,
I'll only clasp thee in my dreams,
   And carve thine image there.

But O these shadows that we grasp
   Tell with prophetic powers,
That this dim world must be our dream,
   And death our waking hour.

VESPER HYMN.

BY ELIZA SCUDDER.

THE day is done, the weary day of thought and toil is past,
Soft falls the twilight cool and gray on the tired earth at last;
By wisest teachers wearied, by gentlest friends oppressed,
In thee alone, the soul outworn, refreshment finds and rest.

Bend, Gracious Spirit, from above like these o'erarching skies,
And to thy firmament of Love lift up these longing eyes;
And folded by thy sheltering Hand in refuge still and deep,
Let blessed thoughts from thee descend as drop the dews of sleep.

And when refreshed the soul once more puts on new life and power,
O let thine image, Lord, alone gild the first waking hour!
Let that dear Presence dawn and glow fairer than Morn's first ray,
And thy pure radiance overflow the splendor of the day.

So in the hastening even, so in the coming morn,
When deeper slumber shall be given and fresher life be born,
Shine out true Light! to guide my way amid that deepening gloom,
And rise, O Morning Star, the first that day-spring to illume!

I cannot dread the darkness where thou wilt watch o'er me,
Nor smile to greet the sunrise unless thy smile I see;
Creator, Saviour, Comforter! on thee my soul is cast;
At morn, at night, in earth, in heaven, be thou my First and Last.

October, 1874.

XVIII.

HEAVENLY TREASURES.

EZEKIEL viii. 12. *Every man in the chambers of his imagery.*
MATTHEW vi. 20. *Lay up for yourselves treasures in heaven.*

JESUS makes a sharp contrast between treasures on earth and treasures in heaven — those subject to corruption, and rust, and plunder — these safe in the Divine keeping, where thieves do not break through and steal. This, however, is what is called a Hebrew comparison. In the Hebrew idiom one thing is declared better than another by being put in opposition to it; and the meaning is, Be not so careful of earthly treasures, which are transitory, as of heavenly treasures, which are permanent and unfading.

The text, then, does not by any means give sanction to the asceticism which some have grafted upon Christianity, nor to that sour contempt of this world, or scorn of its wealth and beauty, which are sometimes thought to indicate spirituality of mind. Unquestionably the more of heaven we have within us, the more we shall see it in all things without us;

so that high spiritual frames will not shut us out from this world, but give it to us in more complete possession, albeit transfigured as the image of the eternal wisdom and love.

At the same time it cannot be denied that the best ministries of this world to us consist mainly in this — that they prepare us to do without them. The most heavenly state of mind is that which enjoys this world the most, and at the same time does not depend upon it for its pleasures. And you could not apply a better test to yourself to determine whether you are carnally or spiritually minded than this; whether you grow more dependent on outward props and pleasures, or whether you are passing into that untroubled peace which could never be broken up, though the props should fall away, and moth and rust should canker all earthly things.

And this brings me to the core of my subject — the solid treasures which the Divine preacher here recommends — " Treasures in heaven." I think this phraseology conveys to many minds no very distinct ideas. They conceive of heavenly treasures as of something undefined, transcendental, and shadowy, not the substantial and eternal things which the Saviour declares them to be. And the reason why many persons put off the claims of religion and clutch at the things of this world alone, seems to be just this inversion of the truth, making material things the substance and spiritual things the shadow; when, as you observe, Christ does exactly the reverse; He makes spiritual things the unchanging substance and earthly things the changing and fleeting shade.

What, then, are these heavenly treasures? We do something towards dissipating the delusions about them when we say what they are not. They are not the future happiness put in contrast with the present. They are not possessions reserved only in some dim and uncertain Future beyond the grave. What is far off in another world will always look shadowy and unreal, and subject to a thousand happenings. What is present and tangible is sure; hence, the worldly man's maxim, "Let us eat and drink, for to-morrow we die." Food and drink are real things. As to what will be after death — that is contingent, he thinks, and hangs on the links of theologic syllogisms. But the contrast is not between earthly treasures and heavenly, as if one were now and here and the other then and there. Both are now and here, one transitory as the summer foliage, the other unchanging as the throne of God.

I. Passing from what is negative to what is positive, we say first, there are *treasures of the mind*. There are what the prophet calls "chambers of imagery." Our life has two great divisions. There is the period when we acquire and lay up the material of thought, and there is the period when we fall back upon it, use it, revolve it, arrange it, and draw it forth from the mind as from a store-house of grand and beautiful things. " A thing of beauty is a joy forever," because he whose tastes have been so purified and elevated as to enjoy any kind of good has stored his mind so far forth with riches that can never fade. This world will pass away from you, but it is leaving imprints which cannot pass away. They whose minds have acquired nothing are poor and wretched in their own emptiness when compelled to be alone, or cut off from external things. But a mind well stored has abundant resources always in the halls of imagery. You remember the case of the Danish traveller, Niebuhr, who lived over amid the furniture of his inmost mind the things he had seen, and enjoyed them more hugely than in the senses themselves, when " the deep intense sky of Asia, with its brilliant and twinkling host of stars which he had gazed at by night, or its lofty vault of blue by day, was reflected in the hours of stillness and darkness on his inmost soul." And perhaps more remarkable yet was the case of that blind old man whose mind was aflame with light just in the degree that his senses went out in darkness ; when the bursting treasuries of the mind within, the accumulated wealth of years, arranged themselves at his creative word, and unrolled in rhythmic order, and sang themselves in the " Paradise Lost," and " Regained," which have charmed the world ever since, suggesting to us the thought that the songs of heaven itself will have richness in them only to those whose souls contribute something to the melodies.

The chambers of imagery! You will find them dark and empty in the hour of need unless betimes you put something into them. And I touch here upon the cause of that total collapse which comes to so many persons during the second, or what may be called the reflective period of life. In the first period, when the sense is keen and the mind vivacious, mere external graces may conceal the poverty within. But all these external graces are to wither like the flowers of summer. And if beneath them no treasures have been stored away, nothing remains but the dreary vacuity and desolation. Nothing has been read which has been reduced to form and order, and ranged along as the furniture of the soul; nothing has been thought out as the product of our own God-given faculties. Nothing has been seen and enjoyed with aught else than the carnal eye; never with that inward eye which the higher culture opens, ranging all things of beauty in the chambers of imagery, there to be a delight forever. There is nothing of all this, and so solitude becomes a burden, reflection a weariness, for it feeds on emptiness; conversation is all about persons, never about things and principles and plans of beneficence, degenerating always into the poorest or the most mischievous of personal gossip. A mind reduced to this condition gives us the most perfect conception of what the hymn calls "the emptiness of things below." Treasures of the mind become in this point of view of vast importance to our future happiness, even if there were no delight in acquisition. O my younger hearers! you who are in the first period of acquisition, if you knew how much is depending upon it, — if you knew that in the second period which is coming on apace, the intellect is to emerge poor and bare, with no resources in itself, and no fitness for the higher intercourse, unless *now* you replenish its chambers, — you would take every opportunity to furnish them well, and

> "In after years,
> When these wild ecstasies shall be matured
> Into a sober pleasure, then thy mind
> Shall be a mansion for all lovely forms,
> Thy memory be as a dwelling-place
> For all sweet sounds and harmonies."

There is the laying up of inward treasures that keeps them ever on the increase. He who aims at the highest usefulness here will put these treasures into his plan of culture. Wisdom evolved from experience, knowledge ever enlarging from plans of reading, observing, and thinking; the chambers of imagery lengthening out into Florentine galleries with every new step of progress, — all these are storing up every day in the treasuries of the mind; and so when youth has passed, there is something better to appear than decay and wrinkles, — precious fruits, golden clusters of it, not subject to corruption, but ripe for immortality. These are conditions for the right building of the heavenly mansion which is to contain our choicest treasures, and whose foundations should be laid now and here.

II. But again there are *spiritual treasures*. These "chambers of imagery" contain something more than intellectual furniture. The fashion of this world will pass away. But it will have left on our minds within prints and copies of itself. What we have said and done and intended, and when and where — all these are sketched on the canvas of the soul and rolled up and folded away for a day of judgment. Hence, Christ says that on that day, for every idle word that men shall speak they shall give an account thereof. So Paul, as I render him. "We must all be made manifest before the judgment-seat of Christ, that every man may carry away from his body what he appropriated to himself while in the body, whether it be good or whether it be evil." It is the unrolling of the canvas in these halls of imagery which is to show our condemnation or our acquittal in the great and inevitable day. We eat and drink, we buy and sell, and we think the past has been buried under the glare of our feverish present. But in some hour of solemn thought, in the stillness of our curtained chamber where sickness has confined us, in the hour of death, perchance, when the doors are shut towards the street, the landscapes of the mind emerge in long array and in vivid light and unroll our past behind us from the cradle to the present hour. Sometimes this is done with such minuteness and vividness of touch as to warrant the belief that nothing is ever lost from the canvas. And this gives us very distinct gleams of the meaning of St. John concerning the dead who die in the Lord. "Their works do follow them," he says. It is a mighty persuasive to well-doing that its ever lengthening Past is to lie on the scenery of the soul and be drawn after it; and it is the condemnation of evil doing that its chambers of imagery are ever filling with those deformities which make up its scenery forever. Good or bad, their works follow them, for they open in the memory a long gallery behind them. "They shall look on Him whom they have pierced," was the condemnation of the murderers; and so it is with all injustice and wrong. The faces of the sufferers, sad and plaintive, follow from behind in a long procession. What we call the pleasures of a good conscience, or the tortures of a guilty one, would hardly exist to us were it not for these chambers of imagery. Sometimes the pictures in them seem to have faded out, or to be overlaid by new and more gaudy colors; but there is an Artist who holds a brush so delicate and true as to reproduce them in vivid outline when He deems it necessary to bring us into clearer self-knowledge and self-convictions; and only the reception of his great atonement through our inward renewal and the dawn of a heavenly life can throw them into the obscuring shade where they will glare upon us no more.

III. But beside all these are the *treasures of faith ;* and please distinguish between the objects of faith, which only inspire hope and expectation, and those which become a present possession, and, therefore, the treasures of the soul. There is Christian truth which is only a theory and a speculation, and which one may hold, along with any kind or any amount of practical unrighteousness. There may be the soundest and most perfect believing, which is nothing but a floating theory that never touches the ground. There are two kinds of Christianity. There is one which floats in the air ; which lives in the discussions, and sometimes in the disputes and quarrels of Christian believers ; theories of salvation which some will tell you a man must hold in order that his heaven hereafter may be secure. There are doctrines about God and about Christ, and about the relation which subsists between them, which may be true and of vast importance, but which, nevertheless, may be only *doctrines* of faith, and not *treasures* of faith. No truth is ours till we have in some sort lived it ; no doctrine of the Gospel has become fairly our possession till it has entered into our vital experience. " If any man love me he will keep my words, and my Father will love him, and we will come and make our abode with him." You might take all the precepts of Jesus out of their connection and away from his Divine personality, and adopt them as prudential maxims of conduct. And why will not that be all-sufficient, and why may we not just as well leave Christ away behind us and out of the account altogether, if only we take his words and practice them as abstract moral principles? Because you want not only his words, but his life that throbs through them; not only the practice, but the spirit thereof; and this comes from obedience and discipleship, for they bring you into tender and blissful relations with Him in whom dwells the fullness of the Godhead. "If any man love me," — He makes an essential condition; for it is the love of Christ that expels all the hatreds and angers, and the pride of life which our moral behavior may cover over, but which we carry along with us until Christ Himself be formed within; and meeting us in the humble path of obedience and discipleship, the Divine Truth and Love, as they are in Jesus, come and make their abode with us. By obedience in the spirit of personal discipleship the doctrines of faith pass from shadowy speculations into golden treasures, — treasures in heaven not laid up in reserve in some far-off and contingent future, but in the heaven whose dawn is in the soul, and out of whose experience of love and peace the sons of God already are shouting for joy.

The Christ of consciousness, as He passes over from the realm of speculation into the soul and fills it with Himself, will be to you, I suppose, a mystical and shadowy conception, unless there is something in your own experience to give it realism and make it plain. But we can make this clear by most familiar analogies. There is a teacher, we will say, who never meets his class; he only sends them lessons and rules of behavior, and a list of the commandments which they are expected to obey, and a description of penalties for disobedience, or of medals and rewards for good conduct. How much do you suppose this lean skeleton of the ideal man will incorporate itself with the minds and characters of those pupils? and even if they try to grasp it and appropriate it, how much of health and glow will this paper humanity be likely to put into them? Do you not see that even the virtues, cultivated in that way, will have somewhat in them stiff and hard, and lacking spontaneous grace and inspiration? whereas, the good teacher in the midst of his pupils, all radiant with personal love, reproduces himself in them, clothing this ideal skeleton with flesh and blood, and making the virtue he imparts beat with the pulses of his own life. A faint illustration, I confess, of the creative power in the Divine personalities of Christianity when we give ourselves up to their transforming influence; of the difference between the Christianity of floating dogma, or of one which has the Christ taken out of it, and the living Gospel, which not only gives you Christ formed within, as the hope of glory, but as the heavenly treasure already won.

Treasures of the mind, treasures of the soul, and treasures of faith, then, are the riches laid up in heaven. They are what we have now and here, if at all; and they are what we shall continue to have when these changing fashions of earth and sense, and this outward circumstance of clay have passed away from us forever. And you are only to imagine yourself without them to conceive what the future retribution is to be. One might well shrink from an application of this subject when we see what multitudes are toiling to acquire, or how deeply buried they are in the conditions of sense and matter. To the outward eye it would almost seem that there are whole classes of people who wear the human form, whose life is so faintly distinguishable from that of the animal, that when the body falls away from them, there will be nothing left; that there is not spiritual life enough in them to "shoot the gulf of death," and come up on the other side. But all progress and discovery, and all the explorations of our own mysterious nature, confirm the Christian doctrine of man's inherent immortality, that it is inborn, not conferred or acquired. I believe in its lands and its deathless dwellings just as much as I believe in the continents over the sea. But the old half Jewish half pagan doctrine of retribution the Church has nearly done with. No, it is not the *wrath* to come that men have to fear. There is no Divine anger to be quenched in blood, and no rewards for factitious or substituted righteousness. There is something surer and nigh at hand that men have to fear, whose culture is only sense deep, and who depend on this outward show for all that they enjoy. For when all this is shut off from them, what is there left? Poverty, destitution, the sandy deserts of the mind, the squalor and the want and the outer darkness of mind and soul. For we carry away with us only what was in the body, and if there was nothing in the body but the soul's squalor and nakedness, these are all which can emerge on the other side. As sure as heaven is not a *locale*, but a subjective condition, so sure shall we fail of it and be in the outside darkness, unless we carry it along with us over the stream. To the multitudes, then, who toil only for ashes or that which will turn to ashes, the exhortation would be, not flee from the wrath to come, but flee from the desolation and the abodes of darkness.

"Their works do follow them." Our doctrine is an ever fresh incitement to the Christian believer whose life is a continuous accumulation of heavenly treasures. Our chambers of imagery should be an ever lengthening gallery reaching continuously through time and into eternity and bridging over the dreaded gulf that lies between. The essential conditions of happiness are given us here; no different ones will be afforded after we have passed over to the other side. Always our Past must follow us, here and through the endless Future, and our Present will be the resultant of all the forces behind us which we have chosen to bring into play. There are two ranges of mountains in Palestine, standing over against each other, on one of which were pronounced the curses of the Law, and on the other the promises and benedictions. I should take these to symbolize our past history. There is a Mount Ebal and a Mount Gerazim in every one's experience, if he has truly had a probation and a history. They rise up in the past, the one blackened and ragged, and with voices of malediction, showing forth all that is painful in our biography and all the crosses and frowns of the Divine Providence. From the other come the promises and blessings. But as we journey on, one or the other becomes obscured and finally disappears from sight. Clouds of oblivion roll over it and hide it. Sometimes one disappears, sometimes the other. Sometimes it is Ebal, black and portentous, that takes up the whole retrospect, flinging its shadows and maledictions over all the future way. Or again it is Gerazim, looming up in splendors made bright in the westering sun. Ebal has gone clear out of sight, and the promises and benedictions come louder and clearer, and fill our whole space with sphere-melodies and prophecies of things to be. We may not annihilate our past, but it depends on our choice which shall stand out bold in the eternal sunshine and which shall disappear in the obscuring shade. May yours be the mount of benedictions, lengthening on forever and forever, over which the Saviour's Beatitudes shall come without ceasing, and the approving voice of the Infinite Father, " Well done, good and faithful servant. enter thou into the joy of thy Lord."

CHAMBERS OF IMAGERY.

CLEAR was the sky and hushed the gale,
That Sabbath day in Grasmere vale,
As if where now her Poet sleeps,
Nature a holier Sabbath keeps :
He lies upon her loving breast,
The hills all watching o'er his rest,
Beside the shore of Grasmere Lake,
In whose still depths, the noonbeams make
Sweet copies of the quiet scene,
Along her banks of summer green.

I found the place of " Green-head Ghyll,"
And conned old Michael's tale awhile ;
And when the day was waning late
I passed the famous " Wishing Gate,"
Where Rydal Water softly flows,
Afraid to break its own repose,
And came where thy tall cliff, Nabscar,
Flings greetings to the Morning Star ;
Or Evening round thy hoary head
Weaves thy soft cowl of sable red.

Blue ether's arms around us flung,[1]
We climbed thy highest crags among,
And pictures there before us lay
Whose charm will never fade away :

[1] " Blue ether's arms flung round thee
Stilled the pantings of dismay."
WORDSWORTH'S *Ascent of Helvellyn.*

The brook from Rydal's silent tide
Went dreaming down to Ambleside,
And in its summer verdure sweet
Lay Rydal Mount beneath our feet,
Its garden-walks and blooming crest
O'erhanging from our eagle's nest.

The Grasmere Lake beneath our gaze
Put on a modest veil of haze ;
The Helter-water's silver sheen
Seemed like a gem embossed in green ;
Far southward, like a mirror clear,
Spread thy broad sheet, Winandermere ;
Coniston Lake beyond, burned through
The misty robe of mountain-blue
Away toward the fringes, where
The mountains melt in purple air.

The setting sun turned Alchemist,
And streams and lakes and lakelets kissed,
And a vast ground afar unrolled
Of green bespangled o'er with gold :
The hills as monarchs stand confest,
A flashing shield on every breast,
While at their feet their treasure shines ;
As earth had emptied all her mines
Of precious ores and gems most rare,
And poured in molten rivers there.

These golden treasures fade — and then
Comes on the solemn twilight scene.
Bright cherub forms in endless crowds
Build stairs to heaven of amber clouds,
And hushed beneath the orange skies

The earth in meek enchantment lies;
While through the gilded haze afar
Comes bravely on the Evening Star,
And tricks his silver beams to be
Ablaze in Grasmere's mimic sea.

But not less lovely or sublime
Are mountains that I used to climb:
No skyey tint of softer hue
Adorns Helvellyn's wall of blue,
Nor does the Day drop sweeter smiles
On Grasmere or Winander's isles
Than those beneath Taghanic's eye,
Where Berkshire's vales and landscapes lie;
And yet thy heights must peerless stand,
Thy glorious mountains, Westmoreland!

For holier charms are on thee shed
Than glories of the evening red.
An "Evening Ode" thy vales along
Breathes as an everlasting song;
An alchemy of higher skill
Moulds all thy scenery at its will,
And hill and vale and lake and stream,
Fused in the Poet's matchless dream,
Come forth anew beneath the skies
That span the hills of Paradise.

And from thy hills I bore away
Chambers of fadeless imagery,
Which clearer rise and warmer burn
When Wordsworth's quiet page I turn,
Who in these typic glories found

"To what fair countries we are bound "[1] —
As if, in mansions of the Blest,
Our heaven might have its golden West,
And all of earth's resplendent show
In still diviner beauty glow.

And He who came — the Incarnate Word —
When conscious Nature knew her Lord,
Clothed the pure heaven his gospel brings
In earth's most rare and beauteous things ;
The harvest fields of precious dower,
The cleansing stream, the lowly flower,
The River rolling ever on
From living springs beneath the Throne,
The trees that fringe the sunlit shore
With rainbow glories bending o'er.

And ever, to his prophet's view,
The Word createth all things new.
At his anointing touch, our sight
Beholds the Uncreated Light ;
Sees Nature's dower of splendors, won
From worlds beyond earth's paler sun ;[2]
Sees the Apostle's creed writ fine
On penciled flower and eglantine,
And "hues from the celestial urn"
On all our Horeb mountains burn.

O Thou, the all-creative Word !
Beneath whom Nature owns her Lord,

---

[1] See the " *Ode written on an Evening of extraordinary Splendor and Beauty.*"

[2] " From worlds not travelled by the sun
A portion of the gift is won." — *Id.*

Give me the mind and heart most fit
To read thine elder Holy Writ,
That when from earth I bear away
The chambers of its imagery,
The hills beneath thy higher skies
As old familiar friends shall rise,
And all of earth most pure and fair
Bloom with immortal beauty there.

XIX.

THE IMMEDIATE KNOWLEDGE OF GOD.

JOHN xiv. 9. *He that hath seen me hath seen the Father.*

THE great religions of the world, some of which preceded Christianity and prepared the way for it, have been more explored of late and better understood. If we study them with any just degree of sympathy with what is true and good in them, we shall be much less disposed than formerly to show them in contrast with the religion of Christ. We shall find in all of them revelations from God, and truths which when obeyed lead to happiness here and hereafter. This fact so auspicious for the hopes of humanity is used for a double purpose in the discussions of the hour. Those who regard Christianity only as one of the ethnic religions, and not a universal one, treat it very much as we do the religion of Buddha or Zoroaster. They eliminate what they think to be false and transitory, and evolving the good and the true, pass on with it and use it in the construction of a new religion which they think more comprehending and absolute. Their position is not inside the Christian system, nor yet in opposition to it; but professedly above it;

Leaving out of it all that modern thought cannot verify, or all that advanced science is supposed to antagonize, they decline to take the Christian name, because they say it is not broad enough. They want a name that covers more, and comprehends truths which Christianity does not give them.

On the other hand, those who find in Christianity what these religionists do not, will receive it as the absolute religion — not opposed to any of the great religions of the past, but the fulfilment of them all. They were provisional and preparatory, and given to educate the race for the fulness of time. As Origen would say, they were the streaks of dawn which the coming Word sent on before Him until the Christ appeared, the central power of all their splendors, and a new sunrise upon the waiting world. The Word was in the world before Christ came, in the twilight gleams that heralded his appearing, by which all the Oriental superstitions were streaked with light; and the Word made flesh was the open day that fulfilled the promise of that early dawn.

You have in these illustrations a clear conception of the difference between the " Free Religion " that declines the Christian name, and Christianity received as the absolute religion of humanity. I only state their relative positions, not designing to argue the points between them except as concerns a single doctrine of faith. The Free Religion eliminates from Christianity the doctrine of a mediator on the plea that the heart craves an immediate approach to God. Humanity, especially in this present stage of its progress, needs no intervention between itself and Divinity, and it is time, we are told, that any second person or sub-deity should retire from the field, that God may come directly to the thirsting mind and heart, and in humanity as in nature, be all in all.

As a Christian believer I should accept this as the crucial test of all true religion. That religion is best that yields God to us in most immediate and ample measure; that religion is fatally defective that yields Him not, and will get no permanent foothold on the earth. And I hold it the distinguishing excellency of the Christian faith that it brings the worshipper into most immediate relations with his God, and I reject the new religion precisely because it takes him out of these relations and sets him afloat, till he drifts away into the unknown, where God is lost in mist or in darkness.

It is a strange misapprehension of the Christian doctrine of a mediator that it offers to the worshipper a sub-deity to come between him and the supreme object of adoration. It does not give you one person in your devotions to stand between you and another person. That the mediæval Christianity fell into this idolatry was natural enough, infested as it was with superstitions brought over from Paganism. That the Christianity of to-day, best represented either by the Unitarian or Trinitarian division, is given to any such idolatry, you will look in vain for evidence.

What is the office of a mediator? Not to put anything between the worshipper and his God, but to remove everything out of the way that hinders their full and blissful communion. It is to open channels of intercourse where none existed before; or if they did exist, to widen them and clear them of all hindrances, that the River of Peace flowing out from the throne shall be unfailing and free. How this is the rich provision of Christianity as found in no other religion, we now proceed to demonstrate.

It is a revelation of God. It is a revelation of man. And as such it renders possible the gift of the Spirit in larger measure which yields God to man in the most perfect atonement.

I. No religion can bring God into immediate relations with the soul unless it first reveals God as He is. The mere guess-work out of our uncleansed human nature will only be a piled up superstition between us and Him. Brahminism establishes no healthful relations between God and the worshipper, because man never comes to his rights, but is merged and lost in the All. Buddhism establishes no such relations, because though man comes to his rights, when we look at the centre to find God, there is a total blank. Parseeism and Judaism assert the rights of both God and man, but never open the channels between them where the River of Peace can flow without hindrance. God is the Omnipotent Father, was the affirmation both of the Greek and Roman religions, but He was only the sublimation of our corrupt human fatherhood seated on Olympus with more stormful passions, and wielding more potent thunders. Mohammedanism is a later Judaism. " God is God," is the identical proposition in whose iteration it never tires. Free Religion prolongs the strain, always in peril of losing all conception of Divine personal attributes, or sinking them to mere qualities, till the affirmation only means, God is the unknowable Force of the universe. The grand affirmation of Christianity is — God is divinely human ; and this is affirmed not in words alone, which might be piled up to the skies without giving us a revelation. It presents a Perfect Humanity in which the Divine attributes are incarnated in the image of the invisible God. Hence the declarations of Jesus, " He that hath seen me hath seen the Father." " No one knoweth the Father save the Son, and he to whom the Son shall reveal Him." Plainly He does not mean that in seeing the Christ we see God with the bodily eye, but that in Him both by what He teaches and by what He is, the Divine qualities are shadowed forth as personal attributes ; the same in a perfected humanity as in the All-perfect Divinity.

Words alone cannot reveal God, simply because all human speech has its roots in human experiences and passions, and therefore has the taint of our human imperfection and depravity. The Christian ideas of justice, forgiveness, love, mercy, compassion, have no equivalents where there has been no corresponding experience, and so they float in air without any roots to engraft them on and give them a resting-place. Hence the ante-Christian objects of worship are heroes deified; the gods evolved from our frail human nature, taking its faults and vices along with them. "God is love," so the missionary tried to teach one of the South African tribes, and they sensualized the thought, and it sank down straightway into lust. Pile up the words as you may, and string out the adjectives to any extent you please, you cannot make them redolent of the Divine charms and glories, because the words can reach no height above the human nature in which they have their root, and out of which they draw their meaning and inspiration ; and therefore, language alone, gathered from all the dialects of the earth, could not yield to human thought the immaculate conception of the Godhead. No, nor could any language floating down out of heaven do it, for angelic words would be untranslatable into our human speech because they have no roots in our human experience and history. Indeed, angels did come in this way all along the ages, and through all the Old Testament history, giving men dreams of a better state, and prophecies of a better future ; and the dreams and the prophecies sank down straightway into carnal conceptions of a temporal Messiah; and never were these conceptions dissipated, and our human thought lifted up to the Divine Idea, until the angel-song floated over Bethlehem, and the star stood still over the heavenly babe lying in a manger. The Divine Word was then not only spoken, but made flesh, and assumed human relations. All those goodly words whereby we describe the Divine attributes, justice, mercy, forgiveness, and love, He has filled out with new meaning; lifting up our low and sensuous vocabularies into the Divine light, and breathing the Divine life into them. They have the taint of our selfishness taken clean out of them. The Christ in the midst of the ages is a twofold revelation. He is the revelation alike of perfect Divinity and perfect humanity, for one is the image of the other copied down out of heaven. He shows us the God we ought to worship, and brings Him nigh, in order that his attributes, though in finite degree, may be transferred to us and we made partakers of the Divine nature and the image of the Divine perfections.

II. But man must be revealed as well as God, and revealed as he is, else there can be no such correspondency between them as to create man in the Divine image. And what is called "the integrity of human nature," and its power of arriving at all necessary truth by self evolution, is a doctrine whose logic fares poorly, whether you examine it in the light of science or of history. Hereditary depravity is not a mere theologic dogma, but a scientific fact, as well established as that of the precession of the equinoxes or the law of gravitation. The lusts and passions, with the cruelties which they engender, and their baleful eclipse of the godlike in human nature, are patent enough to any but our closet theologies, which refuse to see the world as it is. I know of no surer way of judging of human nature than by the fruits it has yielded and is yielding still. Its worth and grandeur and its glorious possibilities I know in the light of Christianity, which reveals our immortality; and in the light of history, which reports the select martyr train who have put on its nobler traits and worn its crowns of royalty. But when you talk of the integrity of human nature, I must look at the masses who grope in twilight, and at a world that groaneth and travaileth in pain together until now. I must look at a country covered with the fresh stains of fraternal blood, holding as its wards millions of freedmen; made such, not through the spontaneous action of a great people, but through the scourgings of the avenging Justice. I must look upon the whole brute creation subjected to the tyranny of man, dumbly pleading for mercy without finding it. "The integrity of human nature!" You mean probably your own human nature, and those of your fellow-believers who occupy the advanced position of the world and see all things in the rose-light of the new age. But how came you up there on that lofty height, and how came you by the light of the new age? You climbed there by the help of Christianity, and you see the world coming short of the Divine ideals only as you judge it by the law of human brotherhood proclaimed on the mountains of Palestine, and incarnate in a Divine Life made a whole sacrifice for universal humanity, and poured out on the heights of Calvary.

To reveal God as He is, is to reveal man both as he is and as he needs to be. The Divine perfections brought down in open illustration amid the corruptions of earth, pour rebuke and condemnation upon them. We are brought face to face with the infinite purity and justice. Before that we were "alive without the law"—alive to ourselves, our pride, our hatreds, our revenges, in whose gratification the old heroic virtues shone forth with such lurid splendor. The commandment comes and we are a body of death. These supposed virtues had the taint of self in them all. We bow before the Divine manifestation. "I am a man of unclean lips, and I dwell among a people of unclean lips, for mine eyes have seen the King, the Lord of hosts." The two inextinguishable wants of human nature are now disclosed — want of purity and want of life — want of cleansing with this body of death moved out, and want of the Divine Life to flow in with new creative power, that the Divine human perfections in their finite degree may be transferred to us and clothe us in the righteousness of God. You may have no such want as this. But remember that multitudes before have been in the same condition that you are, but found in their profounder experience that the want was tenfold more urgent for not being before felt and acknowledged, in order that our native conceit might be taken down to make room for the Divine riches to come in. The Fatherhood of God being once revealed, without any taint from our corrupt fatherhoods carried up into it, the law of universal brotherhood is given also, and the ideal of heavenly society has dawned upon the earth. Man is to be made perfect only as God is perfect. There is not one kind of perfection for Him and another for us, but only as his attributes of love, justice, and power are transferred to human nature, and wrought in it, do we become his children, and bear his likeness. But in our reception of the Divine life and purity, the law of demand and supply holds forever — the thirst must come before the slaking, the hunger before the food.

III. The revelation of God and the revelation of man are preparatory to their direct communion and atonement. They are in order that God and man may meet together, and human nature be cleansed, enriched, and impleted from the Divine. This is the crowning work of Christianity, and the highest boon which it brings. The gift of the Holy Spirit descending in the line of Christian society, not with diminishing but with cumulative power, is the agency, which Jesus foretold, and for which He came to prepare the way. Teacher, Revealer, Admonisher, Comforter, describe its offices and its work in the human soul. It could not come till there was a place and organism for its reception. Man must first be put in right relations with his brother before he can have any such relations with God as will bring Him near. That done, and a true brotherhood inaugurated, the gift was waited for and it came. It came as "a rushing mighty wind" because of the new courses made for the direct agency of God in the human heart. The Holy Spirit is the same in all religions, faint and indistinct when hindered by their superstitions and depravities, full as the noontide when these have been cleared away. In the language of the New Testament this agency is personified, and in the creeds of the Church it has become hypostatized as if it were a person indeed. The reason of this is obvious enough. The word "influence" is too feeble and inexpressive to describe its power, so direct is the action of God within the soul. He comes as with a flaming sword to cut down our flimsy conceits and imaginations, and wound the heart with a sense of its depravity and its need. He comes as with a refiner's fire to burn away the old stubble of unrighteousness and dead works, and to kindle the heart with a new and abounding love. And He comes with a noontide of comfort and peace after the victory over self is gained, and the consecration is unreserved and complete. The subject of this Divine agency and renewal will not call it an *influence*. He is convinced that there is within it a Divine intelligence, and whether in the call to repentance, or the call to duty, or the whispering assurances of the eternal peace, that there is a Divine personality within them all, and that these are not states and conditions engendered and evolved out of himself. They render prayer not a self-excitement, but a perpetual feast of the soul with her God. But in the gospel sense and in the consciousness of the deepest and most intelligent Christian experience so far as I am acquainted with it, the Holy Spirit is not a person in any modern acceptation of the word. It is the inworking creative Divine energy personified, regarded as if a person; so immediately and with such fulness does God yield Himself to the heart in a Christian calling and discipleship. It is not one deity coming between you and another deity. It is the worshipper placed in such immediate relations with the Divine Person that he is brought near and speaks to the soul as Saviour, Comforter, and Friend.

The office of Christ as Mediator, and the supreme value of the Christian Gospel, become apparent. The immediate knowledge of God is the consummation of its power in the gift of the Holy Spirit. The

Mediator puts nothing between us and God, but moves everything that would shut us out from his presence. The Holy Spirit, said Jesus, "shall take of mine and show it unto you." What I tell or show to you about God, He shall reveal and make known to you in your profounder experience. What I manifest to you outwardly, He shall make good to you in your inward beholdings. What I give you addressed to the eye or the ear, He shall give you as the possession of the heart and mind.

A man has been shut up in some prison-house so long that he has come to regard it as a world in itself, and his solitary lamp as all the light there is. Some friend comes along and opens his prison doors and leads him out, and gives him the noon-day sun in place of his taper's blaze, and the whole horizon instead of his prison walls. This is the work of Christ as Mediator. Men had taken their own superstitions as the light of the world, and their provisional religions for the absolute and universal. He brings them out of their limitations, puts the soul into immediate relations with the Infinite Father, and gives her the freedom of all his wealth and bounty. The pantheistic religions and Free Religion running by a swift logic into pantheism, begin by asserting the soul's immediate relation to God. But when they make man essentially divine, consubstantial with God and a part of Him, they abolish that relation except as part is related to the whole. The Christian atonement is not oneness of substance, but oneness of spirit, end, and operation in an eternal friendship. " Henceforth I call you not servants but friends."

We are not to confound the accidental or temporary adjuncts of the Pentecostal scene with the essential conditions of the Holy Spirit and its creative agency in humanity. Its inauguration as the distinctive power of Christianity had its outcome in visible signs which disappear as its currents become broad, deep, and pervasive. The broader and deeper they are, the less of apparent miracle or anomaly have attended it. But it has been an essential working power of the Gospel through all the Christian ages. The Divine Truth or God objectively revealed, and the Holy Spirit by which that truth is kindled and kept alive in the soul, are the two operative forces of Christianity, and have wrought its miracles to the present time. For its power in changing men, sometimes grossly depraved and insensate, into tender recipients of the Spirit of Christ and inspired heralds of his salvation, is its continued miracle, though operating by spiritual laws, and greater than any outward signs and wonders. It is no valid objection against Christianity as it is, or as Christ gives it to us, that it has been mingled with human additions. Its power in clearing itself of these corruptions which hinder the Holy Spirit in its clearest energy; its cumulative force, whether as the objective truth or the renewing grace which brings it home to the conscience and converts the truth into life, is its most divine authentication, and as I read the signs of progress, this was never more manifest than now.

I do not doubt that what I say of the Holy Spirit as bringing the soul into immediate relations with God, and giving it a new and abiding consciousness of his comfort and love, will be spoken to some of you in an unknown tongue. But remember, I am not appealing to the private experience of this person or that. I point you to the stream of Christian history coursing its interior way for eighteen hundred years; the channels which the Spirit is making for itself deeper and broader, all the more effective because more noiseless in its flow. Not alone in the vast enlargement of the Church of Christ, but its growing unity, its larger and more overflowing charity, and its sense of a more deep and tender humanity, are the signs of this cumulative power. You have not felt it? Very likely, because you have not complied with the conditions. They demand a self-renunciation unreserved and entire, and they demand an organism where the Holy Spirit may be received in multiplied measure, and whence the Christ may have a new and constant forthgoing for the conquest of the world. Individual consecration, and that consecration made effective in a consecrated life and calling, are both essential conditions. I will not deny that a man may take his solitary walk to heaven and do good by the way, as occasion offers. But we are speaking now of the Holy Spirit as it floods the soul with a most full and abiding sense of the presence, the peace and the love of God. And I say this is not found in your solitary walk, or on your rock of independence, as it is found in the brotherhood of hearts and minds lifted up in prayer together. It did not single out John and Peter and Andrew, and endow them apart and separate. It was when they were "with one accord in one place," that it swept all their hearts as one human lyre, and so it has been ever since in the Church of Christ. The individual alone and apart may not receive it in full measure. The collective body of Christ coming together with one accord to do his work and extend his reign have always been "endued with power from on high."

PUBLISHED BY
CLAXTON, REMSEN & HAFFELFINGER, Philadelphia.
NOYES, HOLMES & CO., Boston.

THE FOURTH GOSPEL, THE HEART OF CHRIST. By Edmund H. Sears. 12mo., pp. 551. Extra cloth, $2.50.

Opinions of the Press.

"'The Fourth Gospel, the Heart of Christ,' is a book of extraordinary interest. . . . Judged as a volume on its own merits, it is a rich and fresh contribution to the literature of the ages touching the life of our Lord. It is instructive and suggestive in the highest ranges of Christian thought and feeling." — *The Congregationalist.*

"No book of recent American theology is likely to win more notice from thoughtful readers than this handsome volume by Edmund H. Sears, of 551 pages. As a work of literary art, it has great merit; and its clear, rich, and vivid style carries in its flow great wealth of thought and learning with cumulative power to the end." — *The Church and State.*

"This is a very strong book — the work of a powerful and independent thinker; and as an exposition of the Johannean theology, it has probably never been surpassed in acumen and thoroughness." — *The Literary World.*

"We regard this book as altogether the most valuable contribution to theological literature which has been made during the present century, and one destined to exert a most powerful and benign influence on all the churches. For no minister or theological student can afford to be without it, while no one can read it attentively without being profoundly impressed by it." — *Arthur's Home Magazine.*

"One of the most deeply interesting volumes of this generation. It is as much superior to 'Ecce Homo' in power of statement, grasp of thought, and freshness of conception, as that was to the Christologies of average writers." — *The Light of Home.*

"It is a long time since an American treatise on theology has produced any marked effect upon religious thought. . . . But the book of Dr. Edmund H. Sears, entitled 'The Heart of Christ,' is destined, we believe, to exert a powerful influence upon the opinions of thinking men in all branches of the church.

"The argument of the book is cumulative, and one needs to read it through conscientiously in order to feel the strength of its positions. We believe that the interest which it has awakened is likely to increase; and that, while it will lead toward a modification of the theories both of the Orthodox and of the Unitarian theologians, it will tend powerfully to conserve and establish the essential truths of the Christian system." — *The New York Independent.*

RECENT PUBLICATIONS
OF
CLAXTON, REMSEN & HAFFELFINGER.

FOREGLEAMS AND FORESHADOWS OF IMMORTALITY. By Edmund H. Sears. 12mo. New (and Eleventh) Edition, revised and greatly enlarged. Extra cloth, $1.75.

"The 'Foregleams of Immortality' will stand as a lovely classic in sacred literature, and a beautiful inspiration of pure devotional feeling. . . . The best test of merit of a book is when we feel we have been made better by reading it; and while the one now before us widens the field of intellectual vision, and makes solid and substantial the bridge from time to eternity, it quickens the conscience in its sense of duty, and softens the heart with a tender and more celestial love." — *Christian Inquirer.*

"Dr. Sears has done a valuable service to reflecting minds in the preparation of this volume. . . . Nowhere is the argument for immortality more clearly set forth; nowhere are the Scripture facts, which testify to and affirm it, marshalled in closer array, or arranged with more logical consistency. The clear and beautiful style of the author adds new power to the lesson he has sought to teach, and gives added brightness to the page on which it is written." — *Boston Evening Transcript.*

"The other productions of Mr. Sears have been marked by the loftiest moral beauty, in the purest and most elegant diction; but this is his *chef-d'œuvre* in many respects. . . . We know no religious work of the age adapted to make a deeper, more practical, and more gladdening impression on thoughtful and lofty minds." — *Christian Register.*

"Few books have pleased me so much as 'Foregleams of Immortality.' It is full of beauty and truth. The writer is wise from Swedenborg, and has his own gifts besides. I can scarcely conceive of his writings not impressing many, and deeply. I have lent the book and recommended it in England, where the husks of the old theology interfere much with development and growth. Certainly it is a most beautiful and pungent book." — *Mrs. Elizabeth Barrett Browning, in a letter to an American friend.*

"There is much in the details of the volume which is instructive, and especially as regards the reality and some of the features of the intermediate state. . . . The concluding part of the book is entirely new, being on the 'Symphony of Religions,' and sets forth the imperfect but yet valuable testimony of the various heathen religions to the grand truth of Immortality." — *Chicago Advance.*

"A very interesting volume. The author has herein discussed the pregnant theme of Immortality with signal ability, clothing his thoughts in language so chaste and elegant, and illustrating his ideas by such a profusion of appropriate imagery, that the book has all the fascination of a beautiful poem." — *The Swedenborgian.*

www.ingramcontent.com/pod-product-compliance
Lightning Source LLC
Chambersburg PA
CBHW030319240426
43673CB00040B/1220